lonely planet

POCKET BALI

Sarah Reid, Jade Bremner, Mark Eveleigh, Narina Exelby, Marco Farrarese, Leyla Rose

Contents

Plan Your Trip 4

Above: Paragliding, Gunung Payung beach (p85)
Below: Ceking Rice Terraces (p121)

FROM TOP LEFT: ADI DHARMAWAN/SHUTTERSTOCK, ALEXANDERSTOCK23/SHUTTERSTOCK

The Journey Begins Here

I wasn't sure if Bali would be my kind of place, but there was something about the faded photo of my dad on a paradisiacal-looking Kuta street in 1976 that made me want to find out. In 2004, armed with a Lonely Planet guide, I visited the island for the first time. I was mesmerised by Balinese dance in Ubud. I surfed then-uncrowded waves in Nusa Lembongan. I even scaled Gunung Agung after a big night out in Kuta. And I loved every minute. Bali has changed significantly over the years, yet it continues to draw me back, again and again.

Sarah Reid @sarahreidtravels
Award-winning travel writer Sarah Reid has contributed to over 40 Lonely Planet titles. Read her stories at sarahreid.com.au.

CONTRIBUTING WRITERS

Jade Bremner X @jadebremner Instagram @jadeob
Jade specialises in food and drink, culture and adventure.

Mark Eveleigh markeveleigh.com
Mark Eveleigh has authored several books on Bali, including *Driftwood Chandeliers*.

Narina Exelby ne-where.world
Narina is a roaming South African writer.

Marco Ferrarese marcoferrarese.com
Marco is a Malaysia-based author and journalist.

Leyla Rose leylarosewrites.com
Leyla is a food and travel writer, and has written for newspapers, magazines and online publications around the world.

Pura Luhur Uluwatu (p82)
R.M. NUNES/SHUTTERSTOCK

THE BEST

Beach Experiences

In Bali, *pantai* means 'beach', and there's a surprisingly diverse array of options to choose from across the island, from pumping surf spots to calm coves.

Surf or watch the waves from a sun lounger at **Pantai Batu Bolong**, the Canggu area's buzziest beach. (p38)

Escape to **Thomas Beach** (pictured above), Uluwatu's hidden white ribbon reached by a steep cliffside staircase. (p87)

Hang out on **Pantai Kuta**, where you can learn to surf, quaff cold beer, get a massage and shoot the breeze. (p66)

Settle in with a cold coconut or an icy Bintang on the golden sands of Seminyak's **Pantai Batu Belig**. (p53)

Plop your weary self down on **Sanur Beach** (pictured above) and let time slip by while your family frolics in the calm water. (p104)

Let your hair down for the day (or night) at one of **Pantai Berawa**'s mega beach clubs. (p37)

Right: Pentai Kuta (p66)

THE BEST

Cultural Experiences

Bali's temples, or *pura*, are the epicentre of spiritual activity, featuring dance and musical performances that comprise the fruits of a culture with a centuries-long legacy.

See nightly Balinese dance performances – including the popular Legong dance (pictured above) – at **Ubud Palace**. (p124)

The fragipani-scented royal water temple of **Pura Taman Ayun**, near Canggu, is one of Bali's most serene. (p41)

Wander the misty lanes of Bali's holiest temple, the vast **Pura Besakih**, on the slopes of sacred Gunung Agung. (p136)

Clifftop **Pura Luhur Uluwatu** pairs Indian Ocean views and fiery sunset dance performances. (p82)

Learn the story of Nyepi, Bali's annual Day of Silence, at the **Saka Museum** in Jimbaran. (p73)

Feel the freshness in the morning air at **Pura Tanah Lot** (pictured above), the famed sea temple perched on a pillar of rock. (p46)

Right: Pura Besakih (p136)

COURTESY OF POTATO HEAD

Desa Potato Head (p54)

THE BEST

Accommodation Experiences

Whether you need a reset for the soul or a pampering stay, you'll find it here. Unplug at serene retreats perched above dazzling white sands or revel in the bliss of idyllic river valleys.

Discover Bali's artistic heritage at Canggu's **Hotel Tugu Bali**, a series of traditional buildings redolent with charm. (p40)

Experience the perfect harmony of luxury and sustainability at Seminyak's **Desa Potato Head**, with suites and studios to choose from. (p54)

Take your pick of the many peaceful, dreamy resorts tucked in the lush surrounds of **Ubud**. (p115)

Treat yourself to a beachfront pool suite at **Hotel Komune** in the surfing hub of Keramas. (p138)

Designed by artists, Sanur's **Tandjung Sari Hotel** has flourished since its 1967 opening. (p103)

Gaze out over the sparkling Indian Ocean from a poolside perch at a cliffside resort on the **Bukit Peninsula**. (p76)

THE BEST

Surfing Experiences

Great waves of all kinds compete for your attention across southern Bali. Join the legions of surfers chasing the swell.

Find some of Southeast Asia's most legendary surfing at Uluwatu's **Pantai Suluban**. (p84)

Paddle out at **Pantai Kuta**, the vast sweep of sand enjoyed by surfers of all skills. (p66)

Get an impromptu surf lesson on **Pantai Batu Bolong**, the Canggu beach where catching waves is as popular as watching them. (p38)

Slot into the powerful right-hander at **Pantai Keramas**, a black-sand beach in east Bali. (p138)

Hit the sand, or the waves, at **Pantai Balangan**, one of the Bukit Peninsula's more accessible beaches. (p87)

Pantai Suluban (p84)

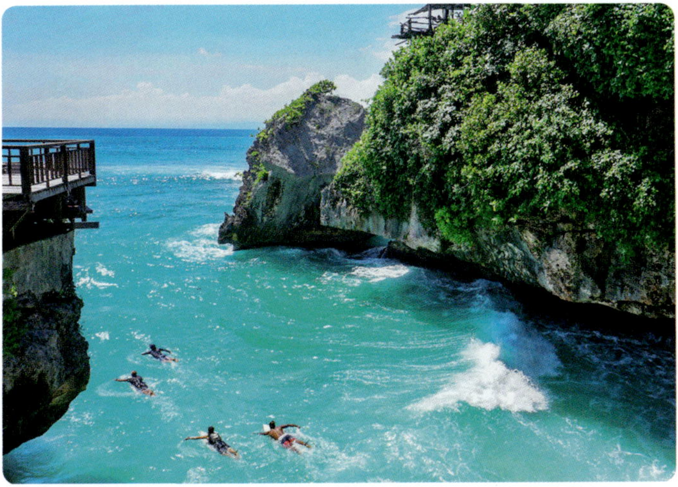

THE BEST

Food & Drink Experiences

Bali's cuisine draws on its bounty of fresh local food, and it's rich with spices and flavours. Savour it at warungs (food stalls) or top-end eateries. Then explore restaurants offering the region's best dining.

Taste the eponymous Balinese chef's passion for Indonesian cuisine at **Home by Chef Wayan** in Pererenan. (p44)

Tuck into a fresh seafood feast on **Pantai Jimbaran** (pictured above) with a Bintang in hand and your toes in the sand. (p76)

Lean into Ubud's plant-based dining scene at **Sayuri Healing Food Cafe & Academy**. (p129)

Drink in the sunset – and excellent cocktails – at **Rock Bar** (pictured above), which clings to the cliffs of the Bukit Peninsula. (p76)

Sip artisan *arak* cocktails at **Potato Head Beach Club** before heading out to dinner in Seminyak. (p59)

Enjoy a tasty evening feed for peanuts at Sanur's atmospheric **Sindhu Night Market**. (p104)

Right: Ledok Nusa risotto at Home by Chef Wayan (p44)

THE BEST

Shopping Experiences

With Bali-born designer fashion boutiques, slick galleries, wholesale emporiums and artisan-run workshops, Bali will fill your bag(s). Leave some room in your suitcase, or buy another one when you get here.

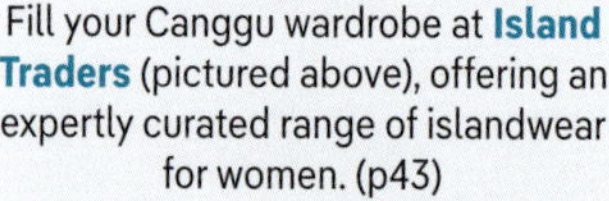

Fill your Canggu wardrobe at **Island Traders** (pictured above), offering an expertly curated range of islandwear for women. (p43)

Find Bali-born fashion labels galore in Seminyak, especially on Jl Kayu Aya. Visit **Magali Pascal** and homewares store **Mercredi**. (p59)

Head to the picturesque Sidemen workshop of **Pelangi Traditional Weaving** for traditional ikat cloth. (p139)

Bypass the big-brand surf shops and proceed directly to **Drifter Surf** in Seminyak for all your surfing needs. Has another branch on the Bukit. (p56)

Pick the perfect coconut at **Pasar Badung** (pictured above), Denpasar's three-storey carnival of vendors and the island's largest traditional market. (p112)

Browse colourful traditional ikat and other textiles at **Tradisi Textiles** in Ubud. (p129)

Best for Kids

Go wild in the aquatic fantasyland of **Waterbom Bali**, Kuta's sprawling water park with scores of thrilling rides, like the Fast 'n' Fierce. (p63)

Start surfing early at **Pantai Kuta** (p66), where patient instructors will teach the youngest of wave-riders how to stand up on their boards by day's end.

Fear not getting swept out to sea at **Sanur Beach**, which has 5km of reef-protected sand and gentle waters to accommodate the smallest swimmers. (p104)

Send the bill to the adults at Nusa Dua's many kid-friendly resorts, and head to the powdery white sand of **Pantai Geger** for a relaxed cool-down. (p96)

Thrill to monkey business at the playground for primates, **Ubud Monkey Forest**. Keep belongings safe while mischievous characters play around. (p120)

Best for Free

Take an invigorating **walk** through a kaleidoscope of green in the lush rice fields surrounding Ubud. (p122)

Hit the beach, with nearly all of Bali's **beaches** currently free to visit. You may be charged a small parking fee.

Be dazzled by the world's best surfers as they take on the breaks of 'Ulus' at **Pantai Suluban**; you can watch for free from the cliffs. (p84)

Watch beach life unfold along the **beach walk** that runs for over 5km from the airport north past Kuta and Legian. Beach bars are tempting diversions. (p64)

Enjoy Bali's best free shows, the daily **ceremonial processions** that shut down streets amid the hypnotic strains of gamelan music and trails of hibiscus petals.

Perfect Days

The secret to enjoying Bali is to slow down and concentrate on one area per day – don't try to bounce between too many places in a short time, as traffic will bog you down.

Pantai Batu Bolong (p38)

DAY ONE

Only Have One Day?

MORNING

Start in **Canggu** (p33) and begin the day with a surf or a surf lesson at buzzy **Pantai Batu Bolong** (p38) before a hearty brunch at **Neighbourhood** (p44). Browse local shops including **Deus Ex Machina** (p43).

AFTERNOON

Visit **Pura Tanah Lot** (p46) at midday for an introduction to Balinese Hinduism. Hit **Pantai Berawa** (p37) for the rest of the day or let your hair down at one of its many beach clubs, such as **Finns Beach Club** (pictured above; p38) or **Atlas Beach Club** (p37).

EVENING

Take your pick from several top-notch restaurants in Pererenan for dinner. Eat your way around the Mediterranean at **Shelter** (p44) or tuck into a seafood feast by the sea at **Hippie Fish** (p44).

DAY TWO

A Weekend Trip

MORNING

Make the drive to **Ubud** (p115). Take in the rice field views as you head up the hills, and begin your Ubud temple exploration at the likes of the rock-hewn **Goa Gajah** (Elephant Cave; pictured above; p126).

AFTERNOON

Have lunch at wholesome vegan cafe **Zest** (p129). Then go for a leisurely **walk** (p122) in the countryside: in just minutes, you'll leave Ubud's crowded streets behind for serene nature and infinite shades of green.

EVENING

Attend a **Balinese dance performance** (p118) at one of Ubud's many stunning venues. Have a late dinner at a Balinese cafe like **Compound Warung** (p128), or something more elaborate at **Nusantara** (p128).

DAY THREE

A Short Break

MORNING

Head down to the Bukit Peninsula and make for **Uluwatu** (p79). Hit the beach – or the waves – at **Pantai Padang Padang** (p87), with surfboards available for rent on the golden sand.

AFTERNOON

Continue on to Uluwatu proper and find a spot on the cliffs to watch world-class surfers tackle 'Ulus' – some of the best waves in the world – at **Pantai Suluban** (p84).

EVENING

By late afternoon, head to **Pura Luhur Uluwatu** (p82), another of Bali's most significant temples. Take in the ocean views and get a seat for the sunset **Kecak dance performance** (pictured above; p82).

If You Have More Time

Factor in a seafood dinner with your toes in the sand at **Pantai Jimbaran** (p76), where scores of seafood restaurants line the bay at the gateway to the Bukit Peninsula. Also make some time to visit Jimbaran's excellent **Saka Museum** (p73) before your meal.

Venture to verdant and soulful **East Bali** (p131) to visit sacred temples and historic palaces, wander terraced rice fields, chase waterfalls and sample local delicacies. Don't miss **Puri Agung Semarapura** (Klungkung Palace; p133) with its beautifully decorated pavilions, and the sobering **Puputan Monument** (p135) opposite the 1710 palace.

Puri Agung Semarapura (p133)

GEKKO GALLERY/SHUTTERSTOCK

Day Trip to the Islands

Just 30 minutes by boat from Sanur, the island of **Nusa Lembongan** (p101) is a popular day trip, and many visitors stay for much longer.

Lembongan's calm main beach is lined with relaxed cafes. Waves break further out on the reef. Neighbouring **Nusa Penida** (pictured above; p137) is much larger and more adventurous, making it better suited to a longer visit. Both islands have good snorkelling and diving, though crowds can be an issue.

There are regular services to the islands by several companies from **Sanur Harbour** (p99). Buy tickets online *(dstarsfastferry.com; return 500,000Rp)*.

On a Rainy Day

No matter where you find yourself on a rainy day in Bali, a **spa day** (p56) awaits, with some of the best spas found in Seminyak, Ubud and Canggu.

Bali's art museums are concentrated in Ubud, with standouts including the **Museum Puri Lukisan** (pictured above; p124) and the **Agung Rai Museum of Art** (p124). There's also the **Museum Negeri Propinsi Bali** (p109) in busy Denpasar on the way if you're headed to Ubud from Kuta, Legian or Sanur.

Malls such as Sanur's **Icon Bali Mall** (p103) and Kuta's **Beachwalk** (p67) also offer rainy-day diversions. Feeling creative? Sign up for a **jewellery-making class** (p41) in Canggu.

Get Prepared

BOOK AHEAD

Three months before Book your resort, hotel or guesthouse to get the best price and the widest range of choices.

One month before Book tables for dinner at top restaurants, especially if you're travelling in a group.

One week before Decide how you're getting to and from the airport. Consider arranging a ride with your accommodation.

Manners Matter

Places of worship Remove shoes, and dress modestly when visiting mosques; wear a sash and sarong at Bali's temples.

Body language Don't display affection in public or talk with your hands on your hips.

Clothing Avoid showing a lot of skin. Don't go topless on the beach if you're a woman.

Photography Before taking photos of someone, ask – or mime – for approval.

Watch, Read & Listen

The Act of Killing (Joshua Oppenheimer; 2013) Documentary about the 1965 slaughter of accused Communist sympathisers in Indonesia (including Bali).

Island of Bali (Miguel Covarrubias; 1937) This classic book on Bali and its culture remains stunningly relevant today.

Ancient Order of Bali (Damn Interesting; 2023) Absorbing and beautifully produced podcast that explains Bali's *subak* system of rice-field irrigation.

Things to Know

Drinks Beer brewed in Indonesia is cheap and widely available. Bintang is the iconic national brand, but Bali's Singaraja is also widely available. Wine and spirits are subject to huge taxes and are expensive by international standards. However, Bali has a burgeoning wine scene and local wineries have some surprisingly good (and affordable) wines.

Sunset From Uluwatu through Kuta, Seminyak and onto Canggu, everybody stops for the nightly sunset show. Some venues like Pura Tanah Lot get wildly over-subscribed. Enjoy the spectacle from the beaches instead, where vendors will sell you a beer away from the crowds.

Apps Load your phone with the Grab and GoJek apps so that an affordable, reliable ride in a car or motorbike is always close at hand.

TIPPING

Bali's wages are low, and while tipping isn't expected, it's hugely appreciated.

Cafes, bars & restaurants

Taxis & rides

Hotels for good service

Guides & beach vendors

DAILY BUDGET

BUDGET: Less than US$80

- Room at guesthouse or homestay: **less than US$50**
- Cheap food and drink in a warung (food stall): **about US$6**
- Beaches: **most free**
- Short *ojek* (motorbike) rides: **US$5**

MIDRANGE: US$80–250

- Room at midrange hotel: **US$50–150**
- Great night out eating and drinking: **from US$40**
- Spa treatment: **US$20–40**
- Car and driver: **US$70 per day**

TOP END: More than US$250

- Room at a boutique hotel, villa or resort: **from US$150**
- Lavish evening out: **from US$50**
- Spa day: **from US$130**
- Car with driver and guide: **from US$120**

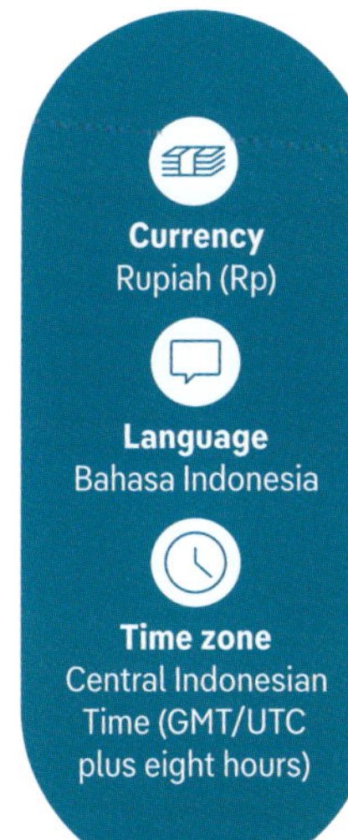

DI STUDIO/SHUTTERSTOCK

TIP

Don't overpack! Bali style is casual, with suitcase essentials including beachwear, something a little smarter for dinner at a top restaurant, flat shoes and sun protection.

When to Go

There's no bad time to visit Bali – there's always a dry place in rainy season and a quiet place in high season.

Being tropical, when it rains in Bali, the downfalls are usually only intense for a short while and are not typically widespread: if it's raining in Ubud, it may not be raining in Canggu.

Overall, Bali's shoulder season (April–June; September–October) is a wonderful time to travel, as the months of May, June and September experience the best weather (drier, less humid). And don't write off the low season (January–April; October–November), as slightly smaller crowds are a plus.

Cultural Events

Bali's special days and events are celebrated island-wide. **Nyepi** (Day of Silence; p67) celebrates the Balinese New Year. It's marked by inactivity – a strategy to convince evil spirits that Bali is uninhabited. The island shuts down completely, including the airport. It's usually around March. The night before, enormous ogoh-ogoh figures are paraded through the streets and then set ablaze.

Galungan celebrates the death of the legendary tyrant Mayadenawa. Celebrations culminate with the **Kuningan** festival, when the Balinese thank the gods. Villages celebrate in grand style. It falls once or twice each year, depending on the 210-day Balinese calendar.

August: Indonesian **Independence Day** is celebrated across the nation, with 17 August 1945 the day Indonesia declared independence from the Dutch. Flags fly high,

Denpasar Weather

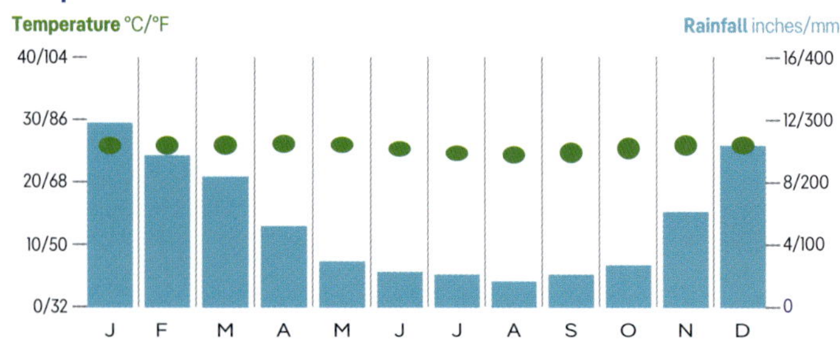

YUN YUNI/SHUTTERSTOCK

Bali Arts Festival

traffic is snarled by processions and fireworks illuminate the sky.

Major Special Events

June and July: Denpasar's **Bali Arts Festival** is the premier event on Bali's cultural calendar. The festival features traditional dances as village-based groups compete fiercely for local pride.

April or May: Ubud's **Bali Spirit Festival** (p126) is a hugely popular yoga, dance and music festival. There are more than 100 workshops and concerts, plus a market and more.

October: Ubud Writers & Readers Festival (p126) is one of Asia's premier literary events and features scores of writers from around the world in a celebration of writing – especially that which touches on Bali.

April to September: When the surf is best on the west coast, there are huge **surfing festivals** and contests in Uluwatu, Kuta and Canggu. The event names (and sponsors) change every year, but your odds of hitting one are good.

ACCOMMODATION LOWDOWN

High season in Bali is July, August and the Christmas holidays. Accommodation rates increase and hotels are booked far ahead of time. To beat the costs, consider areas outside of the Canggu, Seminyak, Uluwatu, Nusa Dua and Ubud bubble; book as early as possible and shop around.

Getting There

Bali's Ngurah Rai Airport is where almost everyone arrives. It's close to major tourist areas and transport is easily sorted. Clearing immigration and customs is now a refreshingly smoother process.

From the Airport

By Taxi

There's no convenient public transport between Bali's airport and the rest of the island. Your options are simple: you can get one of the fairly expensive taxis from the monopolistic airport cartel, or you can use the Grab or Gojek app to get a ride. Once you've entered the airport, you'll wait in a special area for your ride. Note that prices from the many freelance drivers hovering around can often be outrageous.

Private Car

If you've had a long journey to reach Bali, there's a certain peace of mind that comes with having a ride from the airport arranged in advance. Almost all accommodations will do this for you; rates are typically reasonable. Just exit the arrivals area of the airport and look for the driver holding up a sign with your name on it.

How to Zip Through the Airport

It's now easier than ever to quickly speed through the airport's once-notorious immigration and customs queues.

Passport Make certain your passport will be valid for six months after your date of arrival in Indonesia. This regulation is strictly enforced. Also make sure that your passport has two blank pages. Use the automated gates on arrival.

Visa Visas come in many flavours. Most tourists get a visa on arrival (VOA), which is good for 30 days and can be extended once. Apply in advance online *(imigrasi.go.id)* to save waiting in airport visa queues.

Customs Fill out your arrival card online *(allindonesia.imigrasi.go.id)* within 72 hours of arrival and flash the QR code to officials.

Tourism tax It costs 150,000Rp and is payable via the Love Bali app or website *(lovebali.baliprov.go.id)* each time an international visitor arrives in Bali. Currently there is no system for checking if visitors have paid.

Getting Around

Although Balie is small in size, its population and high number of visitors mean that its already inadequate roads are often jammed to capacity, especially in the south, where a short journey can take an eternity. Taxis, rideshares and rides on motorbikes are all cheap. There are no effective public transport options, but walking is often an efficient option for getting around.

Ride Apps

Grab and Gojek are the two top ride apps used in Bali. Both will summon a car or motorbike to your location and then give you a clear price to your destination (tip the driver in cash, about 10%).

Taxi

Bluebird taxis are the island's most reliable, and drivers use the meter. Hail them on the street or use the Bluebird app. You can also book cars through ride apps Grab and Gojek. Never accept a ride in an unmarked vehicle.

Hired Car

Arranging a car and driver for a longer journey (say, Canggu to Ubud) through your accommodation is a good option, and sharing the ride (and cost) with other travellers is a great way to reduce traffic congestion and pay less. Many travellers hire a car and driver for a day of touring.

Motorbike

Motorbikes – everything from small mopeds to retro cafe-racers – are

FROM LEFT: HAND-ROBOT/GETTY IMAGES, WILLIAM'S PHOTO/SHUTTERSTOCK

ESSENTIAL APP

Use your preferred mapping app to find your way around, but don't trust the optimistic travel times.

TRAFFIC TIPS

- If you're going to Nusa Dua, Sanur or Ubud from the airport, ask your driver to use the toll road, bypassing the worst of the traffic. If they're reluctant to use the road because they don't want to pay the fare, offer to pay it yourself.
- Traffic in Ubud's centre can be unmoving, especially at lunchtime. Plan trips outside the hours of 11am and 4pm, and try to get dropped off and picked up on the outskirts and walk in.

easily rented; ask at your accommodation. Congested roads and residents often manically driving their own motorbikes can be overwhelming for inexperienced drivers. Get rides on motorbikes (traditionally called *ojek*) via apps or by hailing. If you accept a ride on the street, set the price in advance (use a ride app to see what's a fair price for the trip).

Walking

Within many areas, you can easily go exploring on foot and get around cafes, restaurants, shops, beaches and more. It's the responsible way to get around, plus it's enjoyable – just watch out for Bali's notorious footpaths, which are uneven and often have hidden hazards, like huge holes. Better yet, head to the beach for a pleasurable stroll away from the traffic.

Follow the sand in Canggu, Seminyak, Kuta, Nusa Dua and Sanur. Ubud is best enjoyed on foot. Other areas with good walks include Denpasar, Klungkung and Sideman.

Dealing with Traffic

The best strategies for dealing with the awful traffic in South Bali is to expect it, don't fret and try to be

Hiring a Driver

It's easy to arrange for a vehicle and driver.

- Consult other travellers for recommendations.
- Ask for a driver at your accommodation, as this increases accountability.
- Meet the driver first and make sure their English is sufficient for you to effectively communicate.
- Agree on the journey and price beforehand.
- Make it clear you want to avoid tourist-trap restaurants and shops, which offer possible driver kickbacks/commissions.
- Buy your driver lunch (but note that they may want to eat elsewhere to get a break from work and your company). Offer snacks and drinks.

patient – remember that you only have to deal with the traffic for the duration of your trip, unlike the Balinese, for whom it's a little more long-term; live local, stay where you want to be and visit what's within walking distance. Also try to keep travel to realistic timelines, maybe turning that day trip into an overnighter.

TRY_MY_BEST/SHUTTERSTOCK

TRAVEL COSTS

Motorbike rental
From 75,000Rp per day

Petrol
Approx 12,000Rp per litre

Motorbike ride
From 15,000Rp

LICENCE & HELMET

An international driving permit valid for a car or motorbike is legally required for renting a vehicle (and likely also for your travel insurance). Helmets are also mandatory.

BALI'S UNUSED PUBLIC BUSES

Trans Sarbagita *(instagram.com/trans_sarbagita)* runs air-con commuter buses, more suited to residents due to the complex route network, although it's rare to see any actual passengers aboard one. The buses are handy for the following routes: the bypass linking Sanur to Jimbaran; Denpasar to Jimbaran; Ubud to Denpasar. Other routes require transfers, and the airport service is inconvenient. The cheap fares require Indonesian e-payment apps.

RAFAEL.LCW0120/WIKIPEDIA/CC BY-SA 4.0

A Few Surprises

Across Bali, the most interesting sights and experiences often revolve around the local culture. It's one rich delight after another.

Ceremonial Offerings Everywhere

Bali's gods, ancestors, spirits and demons are presented with offerings throughout the day as a sign of respect and gratitude. These gifts to higher beings should be attractive, so each offering is a tiny work of art. The most common is a banana-leaf tray little bigger than a saucer, artfully topped with flowers, food and more. Once presented to the gods, an offering cannot be used again, so new ones are made each day, usually by women. The gods are said to instantly enjoy an offering's essence, so the dogs often seen hovering around them have to make do with leftovers.

Traditional Markets

Pasar (markets) offer a glimpse into local life. They're lively and colourful, featuring baskets loaded with fruit, vegetables, flowers, spices and varieties of rice. There are trays of live chickens, dead chickens, freshly slaughtered pigs, sardines, multi-hued cakes, ready-made offerings and stalls selling *es cendol* (colourful iced-coconut drink), *bubur* (rice porridge) or *nasi campur* (rice with a choice of side dishes) for breakfast.

Among the traditional markets to visit are Kuta's **Pasar Kuta** (p68), Legian's **Pasar Pagi Desa Adat Legian** (p68), Denpasar's **Pasar Badung** (Bali's largest; p112) and the sprawling **Klungkung Market**. Morning is always the best time.

Penjor Overhead

Huge, decorated *penjor* (ceremonial bamboo poles) appear in front

OFFBEAT BALI

From May to September, look for huge kites flying overhead; head to Sanur for the **Bali Kite Festival** (p104).

Mysteries abound at **Goa Gajah** (Elephant Cave; p126) near Ubud. Is that a demon at the entrance? Who made it? How old is it?

Tour displays of ogoh-ogoh – huge, cartoonish figurines crafted for Nyepi (p67) – at the **Saka Museum** (p73) in Jimbaran.

Entertaining dioramas depict Bali's resistance to Dutch colonialism at Denpasar's **Bajra Sandhi Monument** (p112).

CHRISTINA DESITRIVIANTIE/SHUTTERSTOCK

Klungkung Market

of homes and on streets as part of various festival celebrations. Designs are diverse, but they always feature the signature drooping top – in honour of the tail of the Barong (mythical lion-dog creature) and in the shape of Gunung Agung. The decorated *sampian* (tips) are exquisite.

Unexpected Museum

An outstanding community-run centre in the unassuming east Bali village of Jungutan, **Samsara Living Museum** (p135) is a real find. Visit the museum for a fascinating window into Balinese culture and daily life, then get hands-on with activities including cooking and *arak*-making classes, *genjek* (traditional form of Balinese music) lessons, offering-making classes and more.

City of the Future?

A world away from Bali's ancient temples, **Nuanu Creative City** *(nuanu.com, adult/child 50,000Rp/free)* feels like a wellness theme park with its serene day spa, butterfly garden, alpaca park and tranquil hotel. But this futuristic and still-evolving 44-hectare development in Tabanan, west of Canggu, has a bit of something for everyone. Here you can also take art classes, admire surreal light installations, party beneath Burning Man–esque sculptures at **Luna Beach Club** and even enrol your kids at an international school. Quirky? Certainly. But Nuanu is never boring.

Explore Bali

Worth a Trip

Walking Tours

Driving Tours

Penglipuran (p135)
KUENLIN/SHUTTERSTOCK

See p44 for eating, drinking and shopping listings

Researched by
Sarah Reid

Explore
Canggu & Around

Surfers put Canggu (chan-goo) on the map, but over the past decade or two, this once-low-key stretch of South Bali's coastline has evolved into the island's most cosmopolitan beach area, home to what may be the world's highest concentration of hip cafes and restaurants per capita.

Centred on Pantai Batu Bolong, Canggu is also a catch-all term for surrounding neighbourhoods, including Berawa to the south and Pererenan to the west, each offering a unique mix of bars, eateries, hotels, boutiques and wellness hubs. Further up the coast is Pura Tanah Lot, Bali's most famous sea temple.

Getting Around

Car & Motorbike

Traffic around Canggu is notorious; on Jl Raya Canggu, it will often take an hour to travel 10km by car. By far, your quickest option to get from A to B in the Canggu area is to use a scooter, whether rented or on ride-hailing apps like Grab and Gojek (you can also book one of their cars).

Walking

New footpaths do make walking easier, but an even better option is to use the beach to get from one end of Canggu to the other.

THE BEST

VIEWS
Pura Tanah Lot (p47)

ALL-ROUND BEACH
Pantai Batu Bolong (p38)

BEACH CLUB
La Brisa (p38)

WELLNESS SPOT
Beach House by Tonic (p39)

TEMPLE
Pura Taman Ayun (p41)

Pura Taman Ayun (p41)
RICHIE CHAN/SHUTTERSTOCK

Pura
Tanah Lot
Jl Pantai Munggu
Jl Babadan
Jl Pantai Pererenan
Beach House
by Tonic
Tyche
Day Spa
Warung
Sika
Luna &
Rose
Island
Traders
Lotus Massage
Therapy Echo
Mojosurf
Masonry
Echo
Beach
La Brisa
Jl Pantai Batu Mejan
Jl Subak Catur
CANGGU
Jl Pantai Batu Bolong
See Enlargement
For more see
Experiences p38
Eating p44
Drinking p45
Shopping p45
0
100 m
Yuki
Hotel Tugu
Bali
Jl Pura Dalem
Pulau
Bali
Teluk
Kuta
Pantai
Batu Bolong
INDIAN
OCEAN

E
F
G
H
0 500 m
0 0.25 miles
1
2
3
4
5
6
18 Echo Silver Bali
12 Samadi Bali
Jl Padang Linjong
45
24 Warung Local
Jl Pantai Batu Bolong
17
21
22
Jl Pantai Berawa
48
Jl Raya Semat
Deus Ex Machina
27 51
50
Jl Angrek
Jl Angrek
25 Body Factory Bali
37
Jl Nelayan
Gang Puji
Jl Pantai Berawa
Jl Pantai Berawa
Jl Raya Semat
35
11 Serenity
14 Zin Canggu
47
Jl Pamelisan Agung
Jl Pantai Berawa
32
30
46
Jl Pantai Berawa
26 Finns Recreation Centre
2 Pantai Nelayan
39
Jl Pantai Berawa
Gang Sri Kahayangan
Jl Pura Kayu Putih
Finns Beach Club 3
Charlie Brown Bali Surf School 9
E
F
G
H

Stroll Canggu

This glorious stroll takes you along all of Canggu's famous beaches, from Pantai Berawa to Pantai Pererenan. Waves and surfers are a constant on your left. On your right, you'll pass iconic beach clubs, mellow family-run cafes, a few temples and even a few fishing boats.

START	END	LENGTH
Pantai Berawa	Pantai Pererenan	3km; 3hr

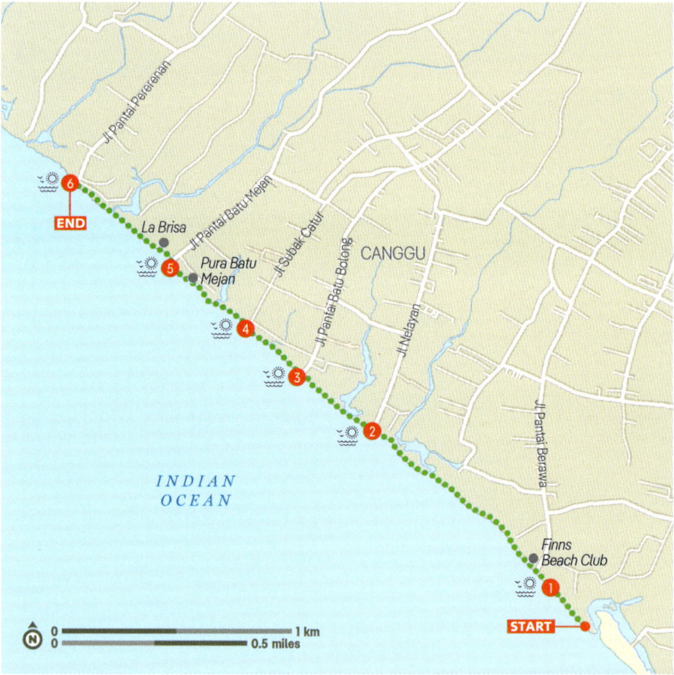

1 Mellow & Wild

The southeast corner of the Canggu area, **Pantai Berawa**, is separated from Seminyak and the south by a wide river spanned by a footbridge. Heading northwest up the grey-sand beach, the bamboo beach cafes give way to the elemental thump and flash of beach clubs like Finns Beach Club (p38) and **Atlas Beach Club**. A cluster of simple warungs (food stalls) past Atlas offer a more low-key option to lounge on the beach with a beer.

2 Find Your Calm

A collection of fishing boats and rustic huts marks **Pantai Nelayan** (p38), a serene (for now) stretch of sand that offers a taste of what Bali's southwest coast was like before the tourist masses arrived. The waves are usually calm here, too, making it a good spot for a refreshing dip.

3 Surf or Chill

Always busy, **Pantai Batu Bolong** (p38) is Canggu's epicentre of longboarding. Umbrella-shaded loungers carpet the sand, and the string of beach cafes and bars is elevated above the shore at the western end. You can even pause for an impromptu surf lesson, with no shortage of local surfer dudes offering their services on the sand.

4 Go with the Flow

Continuing northwest past The Lawn (p45) beach club, the coastline opens up at **Pantai Munduk Catu** and a wonderful sense of space sets in. Ignore the construction cranes inland and revel in the uncrowded grey sand – until sunset, at least, when Canggu's beaches swell with an eclectic mix of locals and tourists and the people-watching is world-class.

5 Surfing & Sunsets

Canggu's most powerful waves break off the narrow strip of sand at **Echo Beach** (Pantai Batu Mejan; p38), watched over by serene Pura Batu Mejan. If you come early enough, you might see local ladies placing colourful offerings at the temple. Take in the action from La Brisa beach club (p38) or one of the elevated cafes and bars lining the shore beyond, which fill to the brim at sunset.

6 Ocean God

A welcome bridge spans the small river between Echo Beach and quieter **Pantai Pererenan**. Note the large, colourful statue of Dewa Baruna, ruler of the ocean, riding on Gajah Mina, the elephant-headed fish from Hindu mythology. Worked up an appetite? Wander up Jl Pantai Pererenan for a delicious feed (p44) at the likes of Hippie Fish, Arte or Shelter.

EXPERIENCES

Surf Canggu's Iconic Breaks — SURFING

Canggu's main break, Batu Bolong is one of the most popular long-boarding waves in the country. Also known as Old Man's (for the party venue just back from the beach), it's a beginner-friendly beach break that tends to break further out before reforming again.

Northwest of Batu Bolong is **Echo Beach** (MAP: 1 P34 C3) or Pantai Batu Mejan, home to several barrelling breaks better suited to intermediate and advanced surfers. Echo Beach Left or Stairs is a powerful left-hander breaking over a shallow reef, Sandbar is the middle section of the beach break, and River Mouth is a reef break.

Southeast of Old Man's, **Pantai Nelayan** (MAP: 2 P34 E5) offers gentle waves for beginners. Further southeast, Berawa has a beach break opposite Finns Beach Club known as the Peak, suitable for beginners on small days. Further out, intermediate breaks called the Ledge and the Bommie work in bigger swell.

You can rent soft and hard boards on the beach from 50,000Rp for up to two hours.

Hit the (Beach) Club — BEACH CLUBS

Beach clubs have exploded across Bali, with more than 50 of these day-to-night party palaces dotting its coastlines at last count. There's a beach club for every mood in the Canggu area. Bounce between 12 bars, seven pools and seven kitchens (serving up sushi, pizzas, Mexican and more) at pulsing party spot **Finns Beach Club** (MAP: 3 P34 F6; *finnsbeachclub.com*) in Berawa, which gets rowdier as the evening progresses. Check the website for upcoming DJ events.

You'll pass numerous other beach clubs as you head north up the beach to **La Brisa** (MAP: 4 P34 C3; *labrisa-bali.com*), which resembles a sprawling bohemian castaway village overlooking Echo Beach. Like Finns it has no cover charge, and with no minimum spend until after 4pm, it's a great option for relaxed day-drinking on a budget. On Sundays, La Brisa hosts a busy artisan and food market.

Go for Golden Hour — SUNSET

MAP: 5 P34 B6

With its charcoal-hued sand and creeks constantly discharging murky water into the sea, **Pantai Batu Bolong** is far from the world's most beautiful beach. That doesn't stop the hordes from flocking here to swim, surf, lounge and stroll by day, with beach cafes, beanbags, sunloungers and umbrellas lining the sand between Jl Nelayan and Jl Batu Batu Bolong. But Pantai Batu Bolong really comes into its own as the sun goes down and thousands converge to enjoy the show. Attracting everyone from local families to shirtless gym bros, it's a great time for people-watching. The concrete stairs in front of the Echo Beach car park are another popular spot for watching the sky erupt in a blaze of tangerine and fuchsia hues.

Learn to Surf — SURF LESSONS

Surf lessons are available on an ad-hoc basis on all of Canggu's beaches, and start from 350,000Rp for two hours. For something more organised, **Charlie Brown Bali Surf School** (MAP: 9 P34 **F6**; *instagram.com/charliebrownbali surfschool*) is on a quieter stretch of Pantai Berawa and wins raves from satisfied clients who show up board-averse and find themselves riding a wave by the end of their first day. For serious students, **Mojosurf** (MAP: 10 P34 **D3**; *mojo surf.com*) runs intensive courses that also include accommodation and transportation.

Begin or Deepen Your Yoga Practice — YOGA

Ubud (p115) might be revered as Bali's yoga heartland but manic Canggu doesn't fall too far behind with its own growing offering of yoga studios. Near Pantai Nelayan, **Serenity** (MAP: 11 P34 **E4**; *serenity bali.com*) is a down-to-earth yoga resort offering nine daily 90-minute classes including aerial yoga. Pop by for a class, workshop or wellness treatment (book all via the website), stay for a meal at Serenity's vegan restaurant, or check into the guesthouse and immerse yourself in yogic living.

You can't stay overnight at **Samadi Bali** (MAP: 12 P34 **F1**; *samadibali.com*), but you can spend all day there. This peaceful yoga and wellness centre (with a boutique, wholesome restaurant and ecoconscious supermarket) on busy Jl Padang Linjong runs up to 15 daily classes ranging from 60 to 120 minutes. Different healers and therapists also work from this dreamy, peaceful space.

GREAT-VALUE CANGGU MASSAGES

Beach House by Tonic

MAP: 6 P34 **D2**

The sister venue of Palm Springs-styled Tonic down the road on Jl Padang Linjong has the same affordable massage prices.

Lotus Massage Therapy Echo

MAP: 7 P34 **D3**

Good for couples, with private treatment rooms for two. Book via WhatsApp *(+62 831 1209 7031)*.

Tyche Day Spa

MAP: 8 P34 **B2**

Sweet little Pererenan spot with consistently good massages for the bargain price of 190,000Rp for an hour, with a choice of coconut, lemongrass or lavender oil.

Find Bali in Canggu MUSEUM HOTEL

Canggu is a cosmopolitan, ever-changing neighbourhood that nowadays feels distinctly un-Balinese, but there is one very special enclave that stands as a bastion of tradition and culture.

Hotel Tugu Bali (MAP: 13 P34 B5; *tuguhotels.com*), a boutique hotel owned by an Indonesian art collector, offers a chance to connect with the history and traditions of the archipelago. Simply walking into the antique-filled property tucked behind Pantai Batu Bolong is an evocative journey into the Indonesia of old, and experiences like Balinese dance, cooking or *jamu*-making classes (*jamu* is a turmeric-based elixir), ceremonial dinners and spa treatments rooted in beauty traditions offer a chance to connect with Balinese culture. Balinese feasts fit for royals *(700,000Rp)* are served in the **Bale Puputan**, housing an extensive collection of artefacts from Bali's 1906 Puputan War with the Dutch (p135). Its street-level **Kawisari Coffee Farm Shop & Eatery** serves coffee from its own plantation, the oldest and largest certified organic coffee plantation in Java.

Dig in to Canggu's Dining Scene EATING OUT

World-class restaurants are now found across Bali, but Canggu has an unrivalled density of cool cafes and international restaurants sporting fitouts as appealing as the menus.

Food quality (and, increasingly, hygiene) is high, and so are the prices – for Bali – especially when you factor in the 12% government tax and service charge added to your bill. And yet the bill for your sushi degustation at hip Japanese restaurant **Yuki** (MAP: 15 P34 A5) or contemporary Mediterranean-inspired feed at Australian-chef-helmed **Masonry** (MAP: 16 P34 D3; formerly Mason) is still likely to total less than you'd pay for the same meal at home.

SURF 'N' ZOOM

Canggu has become one of the world's most popular digital-nomad hubs. While there are some positives – remote workers have created economic benefits for some locals, particularly in the hospitality sector – the influx of digital nomads has partly driven a boom in villa construction that contributes to the strain on Bali's infrastructure. There are nearly a dozen coworking spaces in Canggu. With a mission to create a sustainable future for the local community through its impact program, **Zin Canggu** (MAP: 14 P34 B5; *zin.world*) resort offers a free coworking space next to its cafe, which fills up early. Note that Indonesian law prohibits travellers on standard tourist visas from conducting remote work.

It's not just the food that makes dining out in Canggu such a joy, but the good-times energy that permeates the photogenic venues, many of which host regular happy hours, chef takeovers and other special events. Most local restaurants accept walk-ins, but it's a good idea to book at the most popular places.

Meanwhile, it can feel like a new cafe opens every day in Canggu, most with high-quality coffee and decadently flaky pastries to rival the bakeries of Paris.

Make Your Own Souvenir
JEWELLERY CLASSES

Jewellery-making classes make a great rainy-day activity in Bali, and there are numerous options in the Canggu area.

Guided by an expert silversmith at **Big Tree Jewelry Classes** (MAP: 17 P34 H1; *bigtreejewelryclasses.com; classes from 450,000Rp*) in Berawa, a standard class) will see you shape, hammer and solder 7g of silver (enough to make a ring pendant) to form your desired piece of jewellery, then sand and polish it for a professional finish. Classes take from one to 2½ hours.

Like Big Tree, standard classes at **Echo Silver Bali** (MAP: 18 P34 F1; *echosilverbali.com; classes from 450,000Rp*) in Canggu include the creation of a small piece of silver jewellery with the option to have it gold-plated for an additional cost.

Catch Sunset at a Serene Temple
HINDU TEMPLE

The area known as Cemagi makes a pleasant 20-minute side trip from Canggu and the busy beaches further southeast. **Pura Gede Luhur Batu Ngaus** (MAP: 19 P34 B1) sits atop a dramatic outcrop of black lava rock jutting out into the pounding waves. It has all the classic elements of a Balinese temple, and looks like a mini version of Tanah Lot, which is a further 3km northwest. To the immediate southeast, there is a long series of simple warungs serving drinks and snacks at cliffside tables. Just north of the temple is the black-sand **Pantai Mengening** (MAP: 20 P34 B1), a fine place to while away an afternoon. Like just about everywhere in Canggu, motorbikes are the best way to get around Cemagi.

Visit an Extraordinary Temple
HINDU TEMPLE

Pura Taman Ayun (MAP: 21 P34 H2; *30,000Rp*) is a beautiful place of enveloping calm. This huge royal water temple in Mengwi, 11km north of Canggu, is surrounded by a wide, elegant moat. Built in 1634 and renovated in 1937, it was the main temple of the Mengwi kingdom, which survived until 1891 before being conquered by neighbouring kingdoms.

The first courtyard is an open grassy expanse. The *jeroan* (inner courtyard) is screened by a low wall, which, unusually for Bali, allows easy viewing of the thicket of evocative *meru* (multiroofed shrines) within. The canal-bordered walk around the perimeter of the *jeroan* is a sublime treat. A small museum and an excellent video presentation are included in the admission cost.

Just west of the temple complex, the **Ogoh Ogoh Bali Museum** (MAP: 22 P34 **H2**; *20,000Rp*) celebrates the huge and outlandish papier-mâché monsters that have become a part of Nyepi celebrations (p67).

Feast on Traditional Indonesia Fare

NASI CAMPUR

Ubiquitous around Indonesia, *nasi campur* (rice with a choice of side dishes) is one of Bali's most beloved – and inexpensive – meals, with typical side dishes reflecting the island's rich culinary heritage. There can be as many as 30 dishes to choose from, including beef *rendang*, spicy shredded chicken, grilled fish, fried eggs, corn fritters, crispy tempeh, *urap sayur* (steamed vegetables with shredded coconut), *mie goreng* (fried noodles) and a variety of sambal. Many Balinese restaurants also offer a set-plate *nasi campur* on their menus, but it's more fun to choose the sides yourself. Select your sides and the person behind the counter will make up a plate and charge you accordingly.

Simple warungs cook dishes before the lunch rush. Dishes are replenished throughout the day at busier *nasi campur* spots including **Warung Sika** (MAP: 23 P34 **D3**) on Jl Tanah Barak and **Warung Local** (MAP: 24 P34 **F2**) on Jl Pantai Batu Bolong.

Pick Your Perfect Gym

GYMS

Whether you're in the market for a quick massage or a multiday detox retreat, you can find it in Canggu. But the pièce de résistance of Canggu's booming wellness scene

KEEP BALI BEAUTIFUL

Bali (and the southwest beaches in particular) often receives harsh media coverage because of the rubbish that washes up on the beaches. Some visitors assume that the beaches are permanently filthy, but they're like this particularly during the rainy season, when the rivers carry the refuse accumulated along their banks during the dry months into the ocean. One of the organisations working hard to alleviate the island's plastic problem is SungaiWatch (*sungai.watch*), which focuses on removing plastic from the island's rivers. There are permanent teams that clean the rivers daily, but Sungai Watch also organises river cleanups for volunteers; the schedule is on their website. Another leader in the plastic war is Desa Potato Head.

is its proliferation of destination gyms. A variety of pass types give access to a mixture of a full gym, classes and recovery area (typically with multiple pools, sauna and steam room), and there's usually also an on-site cafe, allowing you to stay all day – and many do. The biggest and best include the enduringly popular **Body Factory Bali** (MAP: 25 P34 **E3**; *bodyfactorybali.com*) on Jl Nelayan, complete with a legs room, sled track, sauna and ice bath. A major renovation of Berawa's **Finns Recreation Centre** (MAP: 26 P34 **H5**; *finnsrecclub.com*) was underway during research, with the new centre set to include multiple training spaces, 25m indoor lap pool, recovery area and other wellness bells and whistles. Rates drop significantly for weekly and monthly passes.

Shop up a Storm

SHOPPING

Canggu's retail game has never been stronger. With no main shopping strip in this neighbourhood, discovering boutiques tucked down unexpected alleys is half the fun.

Canggu's retail strength lies in its contemporary midrange fashion, lifestyle and jewellery boutiques, many of which feature products made on the island. Canggu is Australian streetwear brand **Deus Ex Machina**'s (MAP: 27 P34 **E3**; *instagram.com/deusexmachina.id*) spiritual home; its on-site cafe often hosts live music and other events. Other local fashion and jewellery picks include **Island Traders** (MAP: 28 P34 **D3**; *theislandtraders.co*) on Jl Batu Mejan Canggu for its curated islandwear for women (think: bold prints, sexy swimwear and seashell-inspired jewellery) and **Luna & Rose** (MAP: 29 P34 **D3**; *lunaandrose.co*) for on-trend gold and silver jewellery.

Other notable local spots include **Asasi** *(studioasasi.com)* in Pererenan for stylish menswear designed in London and crafted in Bali, and **Ticket to the Moon** (*ticketothemoon.com*) in Berawa for excellent foldable backpacks and hammocks from upcycled material.

LISTINGS

Best Places for...

See p34 for map of locations

$ Budget $$ Midrange $$$ Top End

Eating

Great Cafes

Neighbourhood $$

30 F5
An indoor-outdoor oasis in Berawa with a vast menu including a moreish kimchi toastie. *7.30am-10pm Tue-Sat, to 6pm Sun & Mon*

Openhouse Cafe $$
31 C2
A somewhat hidden Pererenan location hasn't kept the crowds away from this leafy all-day cafe enlivened by house beats. *6am-10pm*

Milk & Madu $$

32 G5
The Berawa stalwart continues to nail the trifecta of good food, service and ambience. Has another branch on Jl Batu Bolong. *7am-10pm*

Shady Shack $$

33 D3
Canggu's original wholefood vegetarian cafe is still a hit with plant-based foodies, with breakfast served all day. *7.30am-10.30pm*

Relaxed Dining

Home by Chef Wayan $$

34 C1
You haven't tasted Indonesian food until you've dined at the lauded Balinese chef's relaxed Pererenan restaurant. *11am-10pm*

Sista Dumpling $$

35 F4
A peaceful setting overlooking a rice paddy and spot-on *xiao long bao* (soup dumplings) make Sista a great lunch spot. *10am-11.30pm*

Arte $$

36 B3
Dine on great wood-fired pizzas and housemade pasta while admiring the current exhibits by local artists (all for sale) adorning the walls. *8am-11pm*

Yumei Noodles $$

37 E4
The umami-packed spicy beef noodle soup with Sichuan pepper is a solid choice at this Chinese noodle joint. *11am-2am*

Date Night

Shelter $$

38 C2
Superb Mediterranean fare served in an airy garden *bale* (open-sided pavilion), with a special menu for vegans. *noon-midnight*

Ghost Kitchen & Record Bar $$
39 F5
Simple dishes are supercharged with flavour at this neighbourhood bistro, with vinyl DJs on Fridays. *noon-midnight Fri-Sun, from 3pm Mon-Thu*

Numero Quattro $$

40 C4
Elevated neighbourhood Italian fare, with Echo Beach glimpses from the 1st-floor terrace. Try the spicy gin rigatoni. *5pm-midnight*

Hippie Fish $$

41 B3
Fancy Mediterranean-style fish with stellar

Pererenan Beach views. What more could you want? *noon-11pm*

Meimei $$$

D3

The team behind excellent local Japanese restaurant Yuki are onto another winner with this sizzling Southeast Asian barbecue spot. *5pm-2am*

Drinking

Sundowner Spots

Ji Terrace

B5

Sip classic and house cocktails atop Hotel Tugu Bali as you soak up the views over Pantai Batu Bolong. *noon-11pm*

The Lawn

A5

Settle into a beanbag on the sand with a cocktail in hand, backed by DJ beats. *10am-10pm Mon-Thu, to 7pm Fri, to 11pm Sat & Sun*

Black Sand Brewery

F2

It's not by the beach, but there's a breezy beer garden and fab craft brews. *noon-midnight*

Wine & Cocktail Bars

Mosto

F5

Bali's first natural wine bar is arguably still its best. Tasty European-bistro-style fare, too. In Berawa. *5pm-12.30am*

Shady Pig

F4

Experimental cocktails with housemade spirits, syrups and tinctures are the name of the game at this Berawa speakeasy. *7pm-4am Tue-Sun*

Bar Souvenir

G3

The mid-century minimalist interior allows the cocktails and natural wine to shine. In Berawa. *7pm-midnight Mon-Sat*

Motel Mexicola

B5

Begin your night with tacos and happy-hour margaritas at the colour-popping Canggu outpost of the Seminyak institution. *11am-1am*

Bars for a Night Out

Revolver

E3

Rev up for a night out during the daily happy hour (4pm to 7pm). Saturday is party night with DJs until 10pm. *6am-11pm*

Luigi's Hot Pizza

E3

Start with a pizza, stay for the party, with DJs hitting the decks on Mondays and Thursdays. *4pm-midnight*

Gimme Shelter Bali

B1

A rock-'n'-roll bar in Pererenan with a mini skatepark, open-mic Mondays and live music on Wednesdays and Saturdays. *7pm-3am*

Old Man's

B6

Canggu's original beach bar pumps until 1am or 2am. The party then moves next door to Sandbar until 3am. *from 11am*

Shopping

Budget Shopping

Tropicalife

see 

E3

Cheap clothing and swimwear, tropical homewares, souvenirs and more. *10am-10pm*

Canggu Center

C3

Stock up on cheap resortwear, tees, scarves, Balinese art and more. Behind La Brisa (p40). *9am-9pm*

★ WORTH A TRIP

Pura Tanah Lot

A hugely popular destination, Pura Tanah Lot *(adult/child 75,000/40,000Rp)* has great spiritual significance to the Balinese. However, this can be hard to discern amid the crowds, clamour and chaos – especially for the overhyped sunsets. But if you come at the right time and have some patience, a visit rewards.

MAP P34 **B1**

PLANNING TIP
The secret to a visit to Pura Tanah Lot is to arrive before noon: you'll beat the crowds, and the vendors will still be asleep. You'll hear birds chirping rather than buses idling.

Scan this QR code for more information on the temple's significance.

Setting the Stage

Set dramatically on a pillar of rock right offshore, Pura Tanah Lot is the most visited and photographed temple in Bali, but it can sometimes feel like it has all the authenticity of a stage set – even the towering rock formation that the photogenic temple sits upon is an artful reconstruction, and more than a third of the rock is artificial. The ferocious development to the east is controversial, as many Balinese feel that the heights of some of the new resorts disrespect the temple.

A Sacred Temple

For the Balinese, Pura Tanah Lot is one of the most important and venerated sea temples, closely associated with the Majapahit priest, Nirartha.

You can walk over to the temple at low tide, but non-Balinese people are not allowed to enter the grounds, and two sacred snakes are said to live in the innermost sanctum. Follow the pathways in the gardens, along the overlooking clifftop, to escape the crowds and enjoy a more contemplative atmosphere. Immediately west along the walkway is lovely **Pura Batu Bolong**, connected to land by a natural bridge of stone over surf.

SAIKO3P/SHUTTERSTOCK

Practical Considerations

To reach Tanah Lot, walkways run from the vast car parks through a sideshow of tatty souvenir shops, problematic animal attractions and other schlock down to the sea, with clamorous screeching from loudspeakers. Try to get dropped off and picked up just north, at the small **Pura Batu Mejan**, to avoid the scrum.

Note that the pre- and post-sunset rush sees awful traffic, with backups stretching for kilometres. This begs the question, why not just skip Tanah Lot? Mainly because it is an important spiritual place, and the temple and its surroundings emanate an innate beauty. Come long before the sunset rush, and the entire experience can seem magical.

COFFEE STOP

Avoid the marketplace eating options and try one of the cliffside cafes. These aren't the places for lunch, but you can have a morning coffee while savouring the view.

See p58
for eating, drinking and shopping listings

Researched by Sarah Reid

Explore Seminyak Area

Seminyak effortlessly blends luxury with a laid-back beach vibe, and this busy neighbourhood is a magnet for those seeking a fusion of fun and relaxation. While its surf is no match for the waves of Canggu or Kuta, Seminyak's wide stretch of golden beach is arguably the region's nicest. Some of Bali's most-loved hotels and beach clubs are also found here, along with plenty of restaurants and shopping options.

Seminyak merges with Kerobokan – the exact border between the two is fuzzy – known for its homeware emporiums and tucked-away restaurants.

Getting Around

Walking

Footpaths are generally in decent condition, so walking is a great way to get around and explore the area, particularly if you have shopping on your mind. Much of Seminyak's beach is lined with a boardwalk, and you can stroll along the paved walkway from here right through to Kuta.

Car & Motorbike

Scooters are readily available for rent, but it may be more convenient (and safer) to use the ride-hailing apps Grab or Gojek than to drive yourself. Allow an hour for airport transfers.

THE BEST

BEACH
Pantai Batu Belig (p53)

BEACH CLUB
Potato Head Beach Club (p59)

EVENING MEAL
Fed by Made (p58)

COOKING SCHOOL
Nia Cooking Class (p54)

SPA
Bodyworks (p56)

Potato Head Beach Club (p59)
COURTESY OF POTATO HEAD

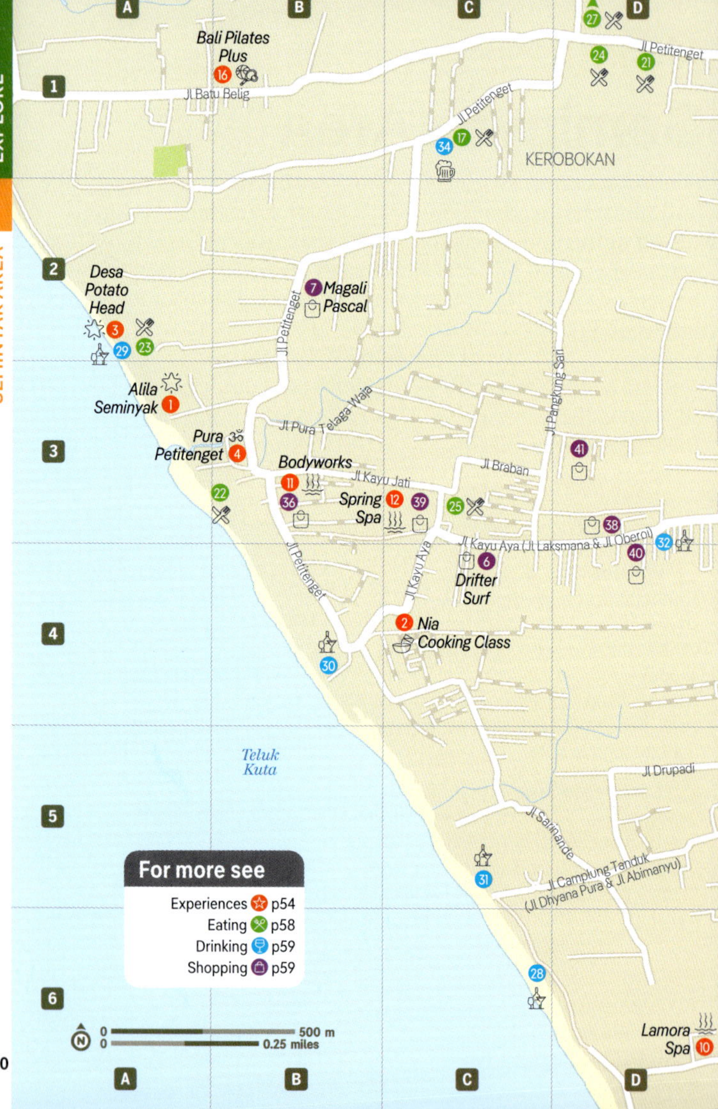

Bali Pilates Plus
Jl Batu Belig
Jl Petitenget
KEROBOKAN
Desa Potato Head
Magali Pascal
Alila Seminyak
Pura Petitenget
Jl Pura Telaga Waja
Jl Pangkung Sari
Bodyworks
Jl Braban
Jl Kayu Jati
Spring Spa
Jl Kayu Aya (Jl Laksmana & Jl Oberoi)
Drifter Surf
Jl Kayu Aya
Nia Cooking Class
Teluk Kuta
Jl Drupadi
Jl Sarinande
Jl Camplung Tanduk (Jl Dhyana Pura & Jl Abimanyu)
Lamora Spa
For more see
Experiences p54
Eating p58
Drinking p59
Shopping p59
500 m
0.25 miles

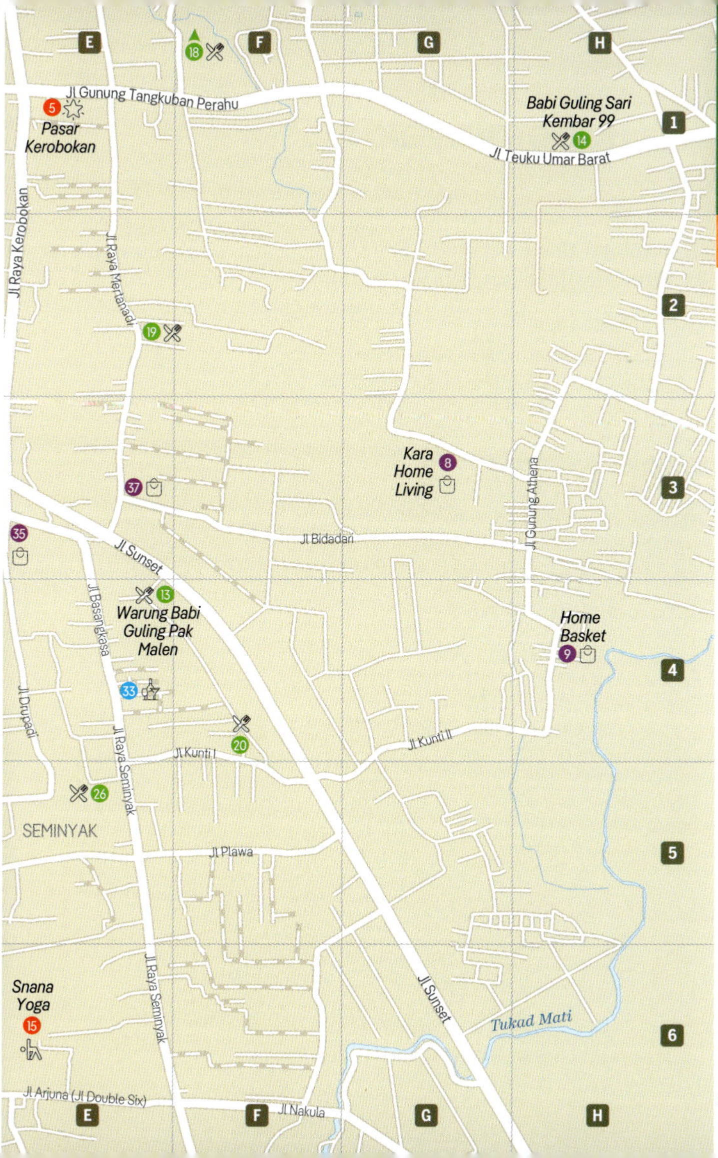

E
F
G
H
Jl Gunung Tangkuban Perahu
5 Pasar Kerobokan
18
Babi Guling Sari Kembar 99
14
Jl Teuku Umar Barat
1
Jl Raya Kerobokan
Jl Raya Mertanadi
19
2
Kara Home Living
8
3
37
Jl Gunung Athena
35
Jl Bidadari
Jl Sunset
Jl Basangkasa
13 Warung Babi Guling Pak Malen
Home Basket
9
4
33
Jl Drupadi
20
Jl Kunti II
Jl Kunti I
Jl Raya Seminyak
26
SEMINYAK
Jl Plawa
5
Snana Yoga
15
Jl Raya Seminyak
Jl Sunset
Tukad Mati
6
Jl Arjuna (Jl Double Six)
Jl Nakula
E
F
G
H

Walk Seminyak

Seminyak's stretch of golden coast morphs from busy Double Six Beach through beach bars, clubs and wide-open expanses to Pantai Batu Belig. Given the traffic, the beach offers more than a beautiful walk: it's a great way to quickly get around – or cool off.

START	END	LENGTH
Double Six Beach	Pura Dalem Segara Bias Saud	3.2km; 2hr

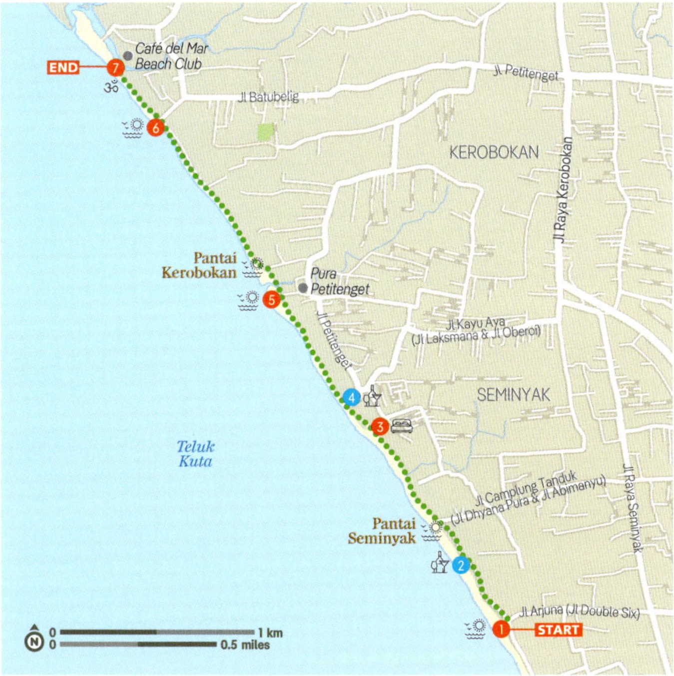

END
Café del Mar Beach Club
Jl Batubelig
Jl Petitenget
KEROBOKAN
Jl Raya Kerobokan
Pantai Kerobokan
Pura Petitenget
Jl Petitenget
Jl Kayu Aya (Jl Laksmana & Jl Oberoi)
SEMINYAK
Teluk Kuta
Jl Camplung Tanduk (Jl Dhyana Pura & Jl Abimanyu)
Jl Raya Seminyak
Pantai Seminyak
Jl Arjuna (Jl Double Six)
START
0 1 km
0 0.5 miles

1 The Liveliest Beach

The paved beachwalk that starts by the airport and runs through Kuta and Legian continues into Seminyak at **Double Six Beach**. There's always something on the go here: students learning to surf, families playing ball on the sand, or couples taking selfies with the ocean backdrop. Beach bars offer all-day imbibements.

2 A Carnival of Delights

Head north along the path towards **La Plancha** (p59). Along the way, you'll encounter vendors selling everything from sarongs and bracelets to speakers, kites and sunglasses. Women wander between the daybeds, offering massages, manicures, hair braiding and henna tattoos. As afternoon transitions to evening, beach bars set up for sunset by pulling out colourful beanbags and stringing lights under umbrellas.

3 Blissful Retreat

The paved beachwalk ends after a tiny bridge over a stream. Now you've reached the beautifully understated and much-copied **Oberoi**, a refined, Balinese-style beachside retreat that's been in operation since 1971. Even today, it remains so exclusive that the beach in front resembles an untouched, private domain.

4 Original Beach Club

Head further north and you'll understand why Seminyak is revered for its beach clubs: the pioneer of the lot is **Ku De Ta** (p59), which has been offering glam beach fun for two decades. The relatively uncrowded sand that began at the Oberoi continues here. Vendors offer peaceful sunloungers.

5 A Sacred Beach

Next up is **Pantai Petitenget**, the scene of regular purification ceremonies, with Pura Petitenget (p55), Seminyak's most significant temple, just steps from the sand. Enduringly popular seaside Italian restaurant La Lucciola (p58) beckons a lunch stop.

6 Coconuts & Surf

Notice the sand becoming darker as you continue north from Pantai Petitenget to reach **Pantai Batu Belig**, a worthy place to pause and sip on a coconut while watching the surf.

7 A Seaside Temple

Finish at the small temple of **Pura Dalem Segara Bias Saud**. From here you can walk the footbridge across the small river to Pantai Berawa and continue along the sand to the heart of Canggu. Another footbridge, behind the temple, leads you over the lagoon to the Café del Mar beach club.

EXPERIENCES

Spend a Day at the Beach — BEACH

MAP: 1 P50 A3

There's a stretch of Seminyak's golden beach for everyone. The northern section tends to be quieter, flanked as it is by big hotels and beach clubs like Ku De Ta (p59), **Alila Seminyak** *(hyatt.com)* and Desa Potato Head, while the southern section, between Double Six and the small inlet near Noku Beach House, draws the crowds. Here, you can rent an umbrella and sunbed and activate holiday mode. Don't miss the spectacular sunsets.

Seminyak's waves are generally OK for beginners, but the shore-break can be a bit dumpy. There's better surf in Canggu to the north and Kuta and Legian to the south.

Prepare a Balinese Feast — COOKING SCHOOL

MAP: 2 P50 C4

Bali's tropical climate and fertile volcanic soils yield an astounding range of fruit, vegetables, herbs and spices. Enrolling in a cooking class provides you with an excellent opportunity to explore how these ingredients shape Balinese cuisine, while also embarking on a multilayered experience that, cliché as it sounds, really is a feast for the senses. Most cooking classes begin with a trip to a local market to shop for fresh ingredients.

At **Nia Cooking Class** *(niacookingclass.com; adult/child 600,000/475,000Rp)*, which is based on the edge of the Flea Market on Jl Kayu Aya, the morning evolves as you set about making iconic Balinese dishes like the delicately flavoured minced-fish mix for *sate lilit ikan* (minced-fish satay). The class ends with a feast – leaving you with a full belly but also a deeper understanding of this wonderful island's culinary traditions.

Plunge into Potato Head — BEACH CLUB

MAP: 3 P50 A2

Like Canggu, Seminyak is revered for its beach clubs, where you can lounge on plush daybeds beside infinity pools and sip on fresh coconuts or tropical cocktails while DJs mix sultry tunes. **Desa Potato Head** *(seminyak.potatohead.co*; p57) takes this experience to a new level. The hugely popular property (which combines a beach club, the Klymax Discotheque nightclub, six restaurants and bars and two luxury hotels) is driven by the ethos 'good times, do good', and from the moment you arrive, you're made aware of how your carbon footprint will be reduced. Learn more about Potato Head's ongoing sustainability journey on its free, 90-minute Follow the Waste Tour, which starts at 11am daily. Sign up online.

Witness Balinese Hindu Traditions

HINDU TEMPLE

MAP: 4 P50 **B3**

Standing guard on Seminyak's busy beachfront is **Pura Petitenget** *(50,000Rp)*, one of Bali's six sea temples built to protect the island from evil spirits. Its name translates loosely as 'magic chest' and relates back to the time, according to legend, the Hindu priest Dang Hyang Nirartha transformed Buto Ijo, a malicious beast, into the guardian of the nearby village. With the iconic *candi bentar* (split gateway) flanked by statues of *naga* (mythical snake-like creature) at its entrance, *meru* (a multitiered shrine) and the intricate stone carvings on the walls and around doorways, Pura Petitenget is a fantastic example of Balinese temple architecture. To enter, you'll need to wear a sarong, which you can borrow when you pay the entrance fee at the southern side of the temple. Outside the northern corner of the temple and standing in a small, manicured garden is a large statue of Buto Ijo.

Discover a Disappearing Tradition

RICE-FIELD TOUR

MAP: 5 P50 **E1**

Most of Seminyak's rice paddies have been razed for urban development, yet some determined farmers cling on to their craft. Intrepid Travel's three-hour hidden rice terraces trek experience *(urbanadventures.com/en/bali; per person US$39)* offers intriguing insights into this disappearing Balinese agricultural tradition – according to environmental organisation Walhi Bali, the island continues to lose 2000 hectares of rice fields each year. Meet your guide at **Pasar Kerobokan** (p58) for a crash course in locally farmed produce (and a chance to sample it) before setting off on foot to a pocket of rice fields that have outlasted the march of development (for now). Along the way you'll hear about Bali's complex UNESCO World Heritage–listed *subak* irrigation system that's still in use today, meet local farmers tending their verdant fields, and learn about the role of the tiny temples dotting the peaceful rice plots.

ALL ABOUT ARAK

Once considered backstreet hooch, *arak* (colourless, distilled palm wine) now features on many of Bali's trendy cocktail menus. Not to be confused with Middle Eastern *arak* (made from grapes and anis), Bali's *arak* can be tapped from more than a dozen different trees, most commonly the arenga palm. Non-alcoholic *tuak* is the juice that is first collected; once fermented, the potent *arak* is around 40% alcohol content. Take care when consuming *arak* produced in village stills, as cases of methanol poisoning (leading to blindness and death) have been reported.

Shop til You Drop — SHOPPING

Seminyak is Bali's original shopping destination, and while an outpost of nearly every brand born here can now be found in Canggu and beyond, it's still a great place to shop.

The main shopping streets include Jl Raya Seminyak, Jl Kayu Aya and Jl Petitenget. The shops on Jl Raya Seminyak are generally a bit more old-school – think batik shops, homewares, cheap clothing and souvenirs. Jl Kayu Aya, on the other hand, houses the flagship stores of several Bali brands. This includes **Drifter Surf** (MAP: 6 P50 **C4**; *driftersurf.com*), a family-run shop offering high-end surf gear and books, as well as the womenswear label **Magali Pascal** (MAP: 7 P50 **B2**; *magalipascal.com*), known for its Parisian styles tailored for the Bali climate. At the big bend in the road before it turns north, you'll find a 'flea market' selling cheap clothes and souvenirs.

The retail cavalcade continues on Jl Petitenget with dozens of boutiques and shops including an Uma and Leopold (*umaandleopold.com*; p59) womenswear boutique.

Kerobokan's Homewares & Handicrafts — SHOPPING

Seminyak has plenty of home-decor offerings, but many of the wares you'll find in its stores are crafted in neighbouring Kerobokan. Going straight to the source offers better value and more choice. Small-scale furniture factories, artisan workshops and retail stores are dotted all over this industrial neighbourhood; more established stores include **Kara Home Living** (MAP: 8 P50 **G3**; *karahomeliving.com*) on Jl Gn Tangkuban Perahu, a one-stop home decorator's store stocking everything from palm-tree bottle openers to shell-encrusted mirrors, and **Home Basket** (MAP: 9 P50 **H4**; *homebasketbali.com*) on Jl Persada with its myriad styles, sizes and colours of baskets.

Rejuvenate Body & Soul — SPAS

You never need to walk far to find a spa in Seminyak. Its spa scene offers a harmonious fusion of traditional Balinese healing techniques and contemporary wellness practices, and there's something for everyone – from budget salons like **Lamora Spa** (MAP: 10 P50 **D6**; *WhatsApp +62 819 1613 2717*), where a one-hour massage costs under 200,000Rp, to ultra-luxe destination day spas.

At **Bodyworks** (MAP: 11 P50 **B3**; *bodyworksbali.com*), you'd be tempted to come just for the gorgeous Morocco-inspired design, but the luxurious treatments are even better, with a heavenly blend of essential oils from Indonesian spices and flowers used for Balinese massages.

Located on the rooftop of Seminyak Village Mall, **Spring Spa** (MAP: 12 P50 **C3**; *springspa.com*) offers urban views with many of its treatments. For a treat, book the 45-minute sunset package including a half-hour foot massage, 15-minute neck-and-shoulder massage and a beer or Aperol spritz.

Get It While It's Crispy BABI GULING

A firm favourite among Balinese, *babi guling* (spit-roasted suckling pig) is prepared with infusions of coriander seeds, turmeric, lemongrass, and other herbs and spices. Many warungs specialise in *babi guling* (look for the image of a skewered pig hanging outside), but **Warung Babi Guling Pak Malen** (MAP: 13 P50 **E4**) on Jl Sunset is a great place to try it in Seminyak. The pork is served as would be expected with a selection of meat from all parts of the pig. Crispy slices of liver and skin, some crunchy crackling, tender meat, and more meat minced and prepared as *sate*. They don't hold back on the chilli, so be sure to order a fresh young coconut to wash it down. People also come from far and wide to feast on the Balinese delicacy at **Babi Guling Sari Kembar 99** (MAP: 14 P50 **H1**) in Kerobokan. Expect to pay around 40,000Rp for a serving.

Observe a Sacred Ceremony MELASTI CEREMONY

One of the most important religious ceremonies in Bali is **Melasti**, a purification ritual performed throughout the island three days before **Nyepi** (the start of the new year, according to the Saka calendar, which usually falls in March). It's the time for sacred temple objects, like masks and Barong and Rangda statues, to be cleansed and spiritually recharged, and they're carried in processions that lead down to the island's beaches. Seminyak is a spectacular place to be during this time, as entire village communities from the surrounding area – all dressed in white ceremonial clothing and carrying colourful, towering offerings and bright umbrellas – gather on the beach in front of Pura Petitenget (p55) for the ceremony.

YOGA & PILATES IN SEMINYAK

Desa Potato Head
MAP: 3 P50 **A2**
The resort's yoga, boxing, athletic training, qigong and meditation classes are available to non-guests.

Snana Yoga
MAP: 15 P50 **E6**
Small, peaceful studio with a 9am class daily and a 4pm class Monday to Saturday. Both run for 90 minutes.

Bali Pilates Plus
MAP: 16 P50 **B1**
Feel your abs burn in a good way at a group reformer class hosted by highly experienced teachers.

LISTINGS

Best Places for...

$ Budget $$ Midrange $$$ Top End

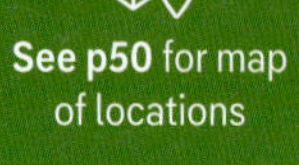
See p50 for map of locations

Eating

Casual, Local Fare

Warung Sulawesi $

17 C1

Flavour-loaded Sulawesi-style *nasi campur* (rice with a choice of side dishes). *8am-11pm*

Pasar Kerobokan $

see 5 E1

Great for tropical fruit and *jaje* Bali (sweet snacks). *5am-10pm*

T&T Chindo's Cuisine $

18 F1

Local chefs rave about the pork-noodle soup at this Chinese-Indonesian joint in Kerobokan. *10am-8.30pm Tue-Sun*

Naughty Nuri's $$

19 E2

A long-time favourite on the island, this high-end warung is celebrated for its signature BBQ pork ribs. *11am-10pm*

Memorable Meals

Fed by Made $$

20 F4

Three Bali-born, Melbourne-trained friends joined forces to open this excellent modern bistro. *6-11pm*

Da Maria $$

21 D1

Neapolitan pizzas in an OTT Amalfi Coast–inspired setting. *hours vary*

La Lucciola $$$

22 B3

Contemporary Italian stalwart with great views from its 2nd-floor tables. *9am-midnight*

Kaum $$$

23 A2

Desa Potato Head's Indonesian restaurant is perhaps the island's best, showcasing unknown flavours from across the archipelago. *noon-10pm*

Brunch Spots

Livingstone Cafe & Bakery $$

24 D1

Prides itself on its croissants, but also serves a deliciously smoky carbonara. *7am-10pm*

Sisterfields $$

25 C3

Seminyak's OG brunch spot keeps pulling the crowds with its all-day brunch menu including a tasty Korean fried chicken burger. *7am-9pm*

Hut $$

26 E5

Lush rooftop hideaway with excellent all-day breakfast, sandwiches, bowls and more made in-house. *7am-5pm*

Nook $$

27 D1

A peaceful garden outlook makes this sprawling cafe a relaxing place to linger; we recommend the local favourites. *8am-11pm*

Drinking

Beach Clubs & Bars

La Plancha

28 C6

Beanbags on the beach and lights strung under umbrellas make this one of Bali's most colourful sunset spots. *10am-11pm*

Potato Head Beach Club

 29 A2

The cracking cocktail list features house-distilled spirits, with food and drink menus designed to minimise food waste. *9am-midnight*

Ku De Ta

 30 B4

Complete with the obligatory infinity pool, plus family-friendly Sundays. *10am-midnight*

Sunset Beach

 31 C5

Popular pool club Mrs Sippy recently opened this beachfront sister venue. Try the signature Golden Hour cocktail. *10am-9pm*

Out on the Town

La Favela

 32 D3

A bohemian blend of Indonesia's jungles, Rio's underground bars and London's art scene. Cover charge 500,000Rp. *7pm-3am Sun-Thu, to 4am Fri & Sat*

District 1

 33 E4

Expertly crafted cocktails are the go at this moody hidden speakeasy. *5.30pm-1am Mon-Sat, to midnight Sun*

Forge Gastropub

 34 C1

A fun place to catch a big sports game, with a trio of local craft beers on tap and a dependable food menu. *24hr*

Shopping

Art & Homewares

Mercredi

 35 E3

Well-made homewares with original designs and a focus on natural materials. *9am-9pm*

Kim Soo

 36 B3

Chic, curated homewares in monochromatic hues. Strong tableware pieces. *7.30am-9pm Tue-Sun*

Purpa Fine Art Gallery

37 E3

Long-time gallery showcasing contemporary works by established and emerging artists. *10am-6pm*

Women's Fashion

Uma and Leopold

 38 D3

The brand's elevated essentials are so popular, it has three stores in Seminyak alone. *9.30am-9pm*

Erica Peña

 39 C3

Need a party dress with wow factor? Peña's bold, Latin-inspired designs have you covered. *10am-7pm*

Lulu Yasmine

 40 D4

The Brazilian-Chinese designer's feminine creations are ethically handcrafted in Bali. *10am-9pm*

Quality Kit

Bali Tailor

 41 D3

Beautifully made leather footwear and accessories for men and women. *10am-7pm Mon-Sat*

See p69
for eating and drinking listings

Explore Kuta & Legian

Researched by Sarah Reid

Bali's original tourist hub may be dated, but Kuta still has its draws. If you're looking for a good beach, cold beer and cheap spas, you've come to the right place – and you'll still find a dose of culture here, too. The golden strip is lined with bars and a pleasant promenade, and a handful of newish hotels make the beachfront more appealing than ever.

Kuta merges into Legian at Jl Benesari. A hybrid of its neighbours, Legian blends the low-key vibe of Kuta with more sophisticated Seminyak. The dining scene is a cut above Kuta's, and it's a short hop to Seminyak for a more stylish night out.

Getting Around

Walking

The urban sprawl and traffic jams make walking the best (and often fastest) way to explore the area.

Car & Motorbike

Ojeks (motorbike taxis) are the nippiest way to get around when you're not burdened by bulky luggage (cheapest if booked through the Grab or Gojek apps). Taxis can also be booked through the apps.

Bus

Kura-Kura Bus *(kura2bus.com)* runs a bus service between Kuta and Ubud. Perama *(peramatour.com)*, which has an office on Jl Legian, also runs shuttles to Ubud, Sanur and other destinations.

THE BEST

SURF SCHOOL
Rip Curl School of Surf (p66)

BEACH VIEWS
Kuta Social Club (p69)

PLACE FOR FAMILY FUN
Waterbom Bali (p63)

BRUNCH SPOT
Crumb & Coaster (p69)

MEANINGFUL SOUVENIR
Theater Art Gallery (p67)

Pantai Kuta (p66)
IGNASIUS MADE/SHUTTERSTOCK

For more see
Top Experience p63
Experiences p66
Eating p69
Drinking p69
Rip Curl School of Surf
Theater Art Gallery
Pasar Pagi Desa Adat Legian
Pantai Legian
Gateway
Legian Art Market
LEGIAN
Teluk Kuta
Pantai Kuta
Pantai Segara
KUTA
Bemo Corner
Pasar Kuta
Vihara Dharmayana Temple
Waterbom Bali
Jl Arjuna (Jl Double Six)
Jl Nakula
Jl Pura Bagus Taruna (Jl Werkudara)
Jl Pantai Kuta (Kuta Beach Rd)
Jl Padma Utara
Jl Legian
Tukad Mati
Jl Sunset
Jl Dewi Sri
Jl Padma (Jl Yudistra)
Jl Sahadewa
Jl Melasti
Jl Patih Jelantik
Jl Lebak Bene (Jl Benesari)
Jl Benesari
Jl Majapahit
Poppies Gang II (Jl Batu Bolong)
Poppies Gang I
Jl Imam Bonjol
Jl Pantai Kuta
Kuta Sq
Jl Bakung Sari (Jl Singasari)
Beach Walkway
Jl Kartika Plaza (Jl Dewi Sartika)
Jl Raya Kuta
Jl Blambangan
Jl Ngurah Rai Bypass
500 m
0.25 miles

★ TOP EXPERIENCE

Waterbom Bali

With 26 slides and attractions in 5.1 hectares of carefully landscaped tropical gardens, Waterbom Bali is a seriously impressive waterpark. But it's not just for kids, with Waterbom's strength lying in its appeal for 'kids of all ages'.

Slide or Float

Spiralling, spinning, shooting and splashing across a tropical oasis in Kuta, the names of the slides alone – Smashdown 2.0, Fast n Fierce, Constrictor and Climax – might convince you that Waterbom *(waterbom-bali.com; adult/child 325,000/370,000Rp)* is for adrenaline junkies. But there's something for everyone here, including lagoon pools with sunbeds and VIP gazebos and an enduringly popular 'Lazy River', which provides sufficient excitement in the form of bridges, cascades and water jets. In 2025 Waterbom opened Zuluu Hill, a new adventure zone just for kids, with six slides across two levels. And while most slides are not wheelchair-user-friendly, Waterbom offers discounts for guests with disabilities and carers.

Feel-Good Fun

A waterpark may seem an unnatural fit for an island with a water crisis, but Waterbom has taken significant steps toward sustainability, with water-conservation initiatives including a closed-loop circulation system, low-flow taps, greywater recycling and more. Waste management strategies have reduced waste-to-landfill to 3.4% and Waterbom was the first Bali tourism site to officially become carbon neutral.

MAP P62 **C6**

PLANNING TIP
Waterbom is open daily from 9am to 6pm. With multiple food spots and bars to keep you sated, you could easily spend an entire day here.

Scan this QR code for more info on rides and to book ahead.

Walk Kuta & Legian

Kuta's beach runs from Tuban near the airport in the south through Legian and on to Seminyak in the north. It's 5km of lovely sand, and the attractions and appeal are surprisingly diverse. The paved beachwalk, which extends the entire length and beyond into Seminyak, is an added bonus.

START	END	LENGTH
Pantai Sekeh	Pantai Padma	5km; 3hr

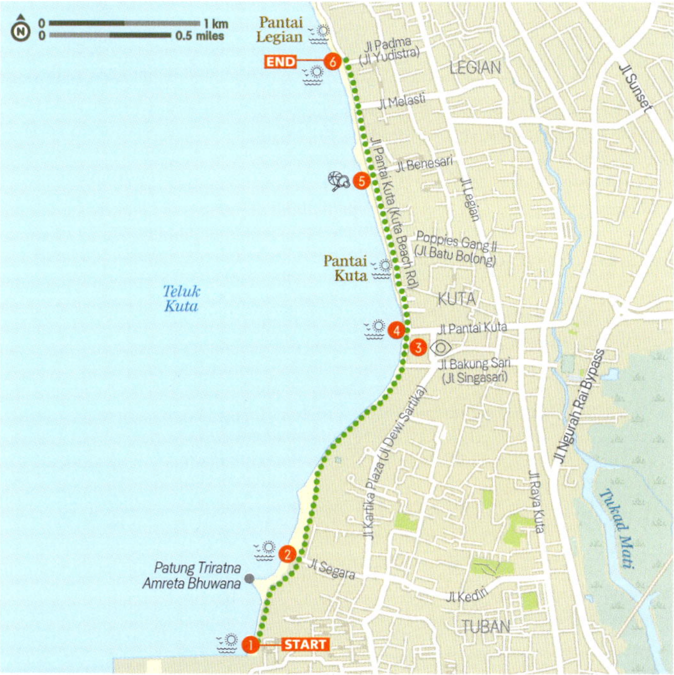

1 Fishing Boats & Plane Spotting

Wind your way along the narrow lane immediately north of the airport's fuel-storage tanks to the little haven of **Pantai Sekeh**, where there are a couple of warungs (food stalls) and a few fishing boats. Head north along the beachwalk as jets roar behind you.

2 Sandy Expanses

The sands here are usually sparsely populated. The artificial beaches reach a point at the soaring, 18m-high **Patung Triratna Amreta Bhuwana**, a flamboyant statue depicting the three forces of life in Hindu mythology. When a tidy cluster of cafes and warungs comes into view, you've reached **Pantai Jerman**, named for some otherwise forgotten German surfer from long ago. This is the main spot for catching boats to Kuta Reef (p66) and other outlying surf breaks.

3 Turtle Sanctuary

Look for the big concrete turtle that marks the Bali Sea Turtle Society's **Kuta Beach Sea Turtle Conservation Center**, which allows visitors to help release newly hatched turtles into the ocean. Eggs are collected from the beaches (saving them from hunters and predators) and then incubated in the sand here (you can take a look) before they're released. The hatching season is usually from April to October. Check online for release dates, and join in.

4 Legendary Beach

The swath of sand known as **Pantai Kuta** begins at Pantai Segara (p66). Along here, it's all about the people-watching, so order a Bintang or a fresh coconut from a beachfront vendor (who will invariably have a sign reading 'bloody cold piss') and settle in for the show of surfers shredding the waves and beginners getting catapulted into the shore break, dogs and children racing each other, and travellers and residents chatting on mismatched plastic chairs. There's always something going on here.

5 Skater Haven

Pantai Kuta isn't all sand and surf. The beachfront **Kuta Skate Park** (p68) buzzes as the day cools down, drawing locals and visitors alike to practise their kickflips, grinds and slides at this excellent skate park.

6 Beach Beers

Pantai Padma – a stretch of Pantai Legian – is calmer and the drink-vendor huts are more substantial, while the sands are less crowded. It flows seamlessly into Double Six Beach and Seminyak. Choose a drinks vendor and enjoy a cold one.

EXPERIENCES

Surf Kuta's Popular Breaks

SURFING

Although Kuta's waves are perennially busy, this area almost always has a wave to offer anyone who doesn't mind paddling away from the crowds. For less crowded waves, typically with less power, go to **Pantai Segara** (MAP: 1 P62 **B5**) on the far southern end of the beach.

Offshore winds combined with a decent swell see surfers with more experience beeline for breaks further out, including the left-hander at Kuta Reef, off **Pantai Jerman** (MAP: 2 P62 **A6**). South of Kuta Reef, **Airport Lefts** and **Airport Rights** break either side of the rocky promontory at the end of the international runway.

Boatmen can always be found on Pantai Jerman to shuttle you out to **Kuta Reef** and Airport Lefts *(return 100,000Rp)* and Airport Rights *(return 200,000Rp)*. The price drops if you buddy up with other surfers. Boats are also available further up the beach, but it's a shorter, cheaper ride from Pantai Jerman.

Learn to Surf

SURF LESSONS

Kuta has drawn surfers in ever-increasing numbers since Bob Koke – Kuta's first hotelier – had his redwood boards shipped here from Hawaii in the early 1930s. These days, with rental boards available by the hundreds and surf instructors by the score, **Pantai Kuta** (Kuta Beach; MAP: 3 P62 **B4**) is one of the best places in Bali to learn how to surf. You simply need to approach one of the board-rental kiosks on the beach to set up a lesson; expect to pay around 250,000Rp for a 60-minute private session. Or engage the expert coaches from the **Rip Curl School of Surf** (MAP: 4 P62 **A1**; *ripcurlschoolofcurf.com; 2hr lesson 722,500Rp*), which has booths in Kuta (inside the Mamaka by Ovolo hotel) and Legian (on the boardwalk south of Jl Arjuna).

Visit an Unexpected Temple

BUDDHIST TEMPLE

MAP: 5 P62 **D5**

Despite its location on busy Jl Blambangan, **Vihara Dharmayan Temple** is quite possibly the most colourful – and calming – place in Kuta.

Dating from 1876, the Chinese Buddhist temple's *Baktisala* (main prayer hall) is adorned with large Chinese lanterns and supported by giant crimson pillars adorned with menacing dragons. Incense swirls around the moodily lit interior. Several small shrines rise up behind the main altar, where devotees leave Balinese-style offerings.

The temple is open from 9am to 8pm. Ensure your shoulders and knees are covered before entering.

Watch a Monster Parade NYEPI

The beginning of the Balinese year, according to the Saka calendar (p73), is **Nyepi**, a remarkable time to be on the island – a day when everything comes to a standstill and Bali descends into silence. Roads close, lights and even mobile networks are turned off, no fires can be lit and even the airport shuts.

The night before, however, pandemonium reigns as enormous effigies of monsters and demons from Balinese mythology are paraded through Bali's streets. The effigies, called ogoh-ogoh, are astounding pieces of art, often standing more than 3m tall. Kuta hosts one of the island's rowdiest and most impressive parades, with huge crowds converging to watch terrifying ogoh-ogoh paraded along Jl Legian. After the parades, the ogoh-ogoh are ritually burned, symbolising the destruction of evil and restoring good energy for the year ahead. Nyepi typically falls in March.

Find the Perfect Souvenir SHOPPING

The art markets of Kuta and Legian aren't what they used to be. While you can still find paintings and wood carvings at the **Legian Art Market** (MAP: 6 P62 **B3**) on Jl Melasti, these markets are better suited to picking up cheap, low-quality souvenirs. Unless prices are set, you'll be expected to bargain; take a friendly approach and don't drive the seller into the ground.

For more meaningful souvenirs with a sense of place, check out **Theater Art Gallery** (also known as Bali Puppet; MAP: 7 P62 **B1**; *balipuppet.com*) in Legian, which specialises in vintage and reproduction *wayang* puppets used in traditional Balinese theatre. It also sells vintage masks, hand-painted batik, decorative ornaments and more.

For high-street brands, head to the **Beachwalk** *(beachwalkbali.com)* mall on Kuta Beach, or to Jl Legian.

MEMORIAL WALL

The bombings on 12 October 2002 are regarded as the worst terrorist event in Bali's modern history. Just after 11pm a bomb exploded at Paddy's Pub, a Kuta bar popular with backpackers, and as revellers fled to apparent safety on the street, another (bigger) bomb was detonated over the road, just outside Sari Club. The blasts killed 202 people, among them 38 Indonesians, 88 Australians and 23 Britons. There is now a **memorial wall** for those who lost their lives on Jl Legian, just metres from where Sari Club once stood. The victims' names are listed, and family and friends still bring flowers and photos to honour their memory.

Catch the Sunset Show SUNSET

MAP: 8 P62 **A2**

West-facing Pantai Kuta (p66) and **Pantai Legian** are famous for dramatic sunsets, and you could write an entire book about the activity that unfolds on this action-packed swath of sand. Along here it's all about people-watching, so order a beer or a fresh coconut from a beachfront vendor and settle in for the show. Watching the sunset here can turn into a static spa and shopping spree – without having to move from your seat you could have your hair braided, get a fake tattoo, and enjoy a manicure and back massage, all at the same time. From wandering hawkers you can buy kites, jewellery, sarongs and more, and there's a never-ending procession of snacks and refreshments. In Kuta, there's also a **skate park** *(8am-10pm)* that has become a favourite meeting place for kids of all ages, with skateboards available for hire.

Get a Taste of Local Life MARKETS

Kuta and Legian might feel far from 'traditional' Bali, but a trip to a morning food market will reveal a slice of life that's remained almost unchanged for generations. Two morning markets in the area are worth a visit: the popular one in Legian, **Pasar Pagi Desa Adat Legian** (MAP: 9 P62 **C1**), and the even more timeless **Pasar Kuta** (MAP: 10 P62 **D5**). Legian's morning market is located in a large, modern building, while Kuta's more colourful market is in a ramshackle shelter down an alleyway. If you're squeamish, avoid the butcher's section where meat and fresh fish are carved up. The most lively sections of both markets are the fruit-and-vegetable stands and the wonderfully colourful stalls that sell a mind-boggling selection of traditional offerings. Look out for stalls where women sell *jamu* – this traditional turmeric-based elixir is a wonderful early-morning pick-me-up. Arrive early to see the markets at their most vibrant.

Admire Striking Gateways ARCHITECTURE

MAP: 11 P62 **B3**

If you enter Pantai Legian from Jl Melasti, you'll walk through an ornate split **gateway** (called *candi bentar*) – the same sort of architectural structure you'll see at entrances to sacred sites around Bali. These traditional gateways serve as important cultural and spiritual symbols, and consist of two symmetrical pillars connected by a central opening, which creates a striking entryway. The gates are typically adorned with intricate carvings and decorative motifs, and represent the division between the profane world and the sacred realm, signifying the transition from the mundane to the divine. The inside edge of the gates are always smooth; some say to cleanse the mind upon entry. See if it works for you.

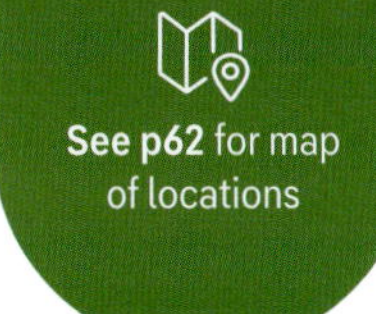

Best Places for...

$ Budget $$ Midrange $$$ Top End

Eating

Cheap & Local

Warung Kampung $
12 B3
Airy Legian spot serving popular, tasty Indo dishes at very budget-friendly prices. *10am-10pm*

Made's Warung $$
13 C5
Turning out some of Kuta's best Balinese food since 1969, with an additional location in Seminyak. *10am-9pm*

International Dining

Crumb & Coaster $$
14 C4
Kuta's coolest cafe spills out of an industrial space, with brekkie served until 6pm. A wider menu is available from lunchtime. *7.30am-11pm*

Poppies Restaurant $$
15 C5
Soak up the old-school Kuta nostalgia at this longstanding international restaurant in a peaceful garden. *8am-11pm*

Fat Chow $$
16 B4
Delicious Asian fusion dishes include a refreshing caramelised-pork-belly salad with shredded mango. *10am-10pm*

Mama's German Restaurant $$
17 C3
Serving up German classics from currywurst to pork knuckle since 1985, Mama's is a Legian institution. *24hr*

Don Juan Mexican Restaurant & Bar $$
18 C5
Watch the world go by on Jl Pantai Kuta while you munch on tacos and sip margaritas. *8am-11.30pm*

Drinking

Seaside Drinks

Kanoa Bali
19 B2
The smartest beach bar on the Legian strip, with wine by the glass, local beers and spicy passion-fruit margaritas. *7am-10pm*

Kuta Social Club
20 B3
A relaxed rooftop pool club with Mediterranean-inspired dishes, colourful cocktails and views to the Bukit. *7am-11.30pm*

Double-Six Rooftop Sunset Bar
21 A1
Settle into a daybed surrounded by an infinity pond at one of Bali's largest rooftop bars. *5-11pm*

Having a Few

Sky Garden Bali
22 C4
Kuta's only mega club pumps every night; reserve ahead for a semi-private party area. *9pm-4am*

PaD Bar & Grill
23 C3
Come for a cheap feed and stay for the party atmosphere, with regular drag shows. Also screens sports. *7.30am-11.30pm*

See p77
for eating and drinking listings

Explore Jimbaran

Researched by Jade Bremner

Teluk Jimbaran (Jimbaran Bay) sits south of the international airport but feels miles away, with its pristine white-sandy beach stretching 4km in length. Every night at sunset, the adjacent string of seafood restaurants draws diners to sample the grilled treats. At the south end, the landmark Four Seasons Jimbaran Bay rises up a bushy headland; other discreet resorts are set back from the beach. Nearby attractions include the towering Patung Garuda Wisnu Kencana statue, one of the world's tallest, and the first of the Bukit Peninsula's lovely coves. Jimbaran is often overlooked by visitors intent on the delights of Uluwatu, but this waterfront village offers a fascinating glimpse into local life.

Getting Around

Taxi

Immediately south of the airport, you can't beat the access, especially if you have a late-arriving or early-departing flight. Access from the north means missing the worst of the Bukit Peninsula traffic – another plus. Innumerable cabs, Grabs and Gojeks can be found near the seafood restaurants.

Walking

The areas around Pantai Jimbaran are easy to navigate by foot along the sand or a block back from the sea next to the seafood restaurants, where there are stretches of pavement.

THE BEST

BEACH
Pantai Jimbaran (p76)

SEAFOOD RESTAURANTS
Queen Beach (p76)

MUSEUM
Saka Museum (p73)

DRAMATIC VIEWS
Rock Bar (p76)

DAY OUT
GWK Cultural Park (p76)

Pantai Jimbaran (p76)
FIKY AGUS SETIAWAN/SHUTTERSTOCK

A
B
C
D
1
2
3
4
5
6
500 m
0.25 miles
For more see
Top Experience p73
Experiences p76
Eating p77
Drinking p77
Teluk Jimbaran
Pantai Kedonganan
KEDONGANAN
Jl Pasir Putih
Jl Toya Ning
Jl Pantai Kedonganan
Jl Pengeracikan
Jl Pemelisan
Jl Segara Wangi
Jl Uluwatu
I Gusti Ngurah Rai International (3.5km)
Teluk Kuta
Rock Bar
See Main Map
Saka Museum
1 km
0.5 miles
Jl Batas Kauh
Pantai Jimbaran
Jl Pantai Jimbaran
Jl Pemelisan Agung
Queen Beach
Jl Ulunsiwi
Jl Ngurah Rai Bypass
Jl Yoga Perkanti
Jimbaran Beach
Teluk Benoa
Map continues in Inset
JIMBARAN
Pantai Muaya
Jl Bukit Permai
Jl Uluwatu II

★ TOP EXPERIENCE

Saka Museum

Enormous effigies of ogoh-ogoh, the demons of Balinese mythology, are paraded through the streets for Balinese New Year the night before Nyepi, Bali's Day of Silence. Saka Museum delves into this cultural phenomenon.

The Saka Calendar

The museum holds old examples of the Saka calendar (78 years behind the Gregorian calendar), plus cultural relics from silk scarves to intricate jewellery relating to the five elements connected with the solar and lunar calendars.

Day of Silence

Nyepi is when everything comes to a standstill and the island descends into silence. Photos in exhibition halls account for this remarkable tradition.

Roads are closed, lights are turned off and no fires can be made. Even the airspace over Bali is shut. The night before (Pengrupukan), however, is absolute pandemonium, as enormous effigies of monsters are paraded around.

Walking among Giants

Visitors can view the giant-sized ogoh-ogoh figures, astounding bamboo and papier-mâché effigies that often stand over 3m tall. These fearsome monsters are paraded through the streets to ward off evil spirits, as musical instruments are banged, clattered and beaten. Kids and grown-ups alike will love staring at these menacing depictions of characters from Hindu myth, with their bulbous eyes, sharp teeth and long tongues.

MAP P72 **A3**

PLANNING TIP
Save time for the 3rd floor's Saka Auditorium, which shows 360-degree movies of Bali scenes in a tented dome theatre. A small cafe on the 1st floor serves teas and coffees.

Scan this QR code to get tickets in advance

WALKING TOUR

Walk Jimbaran

This walk, taking in Jimbaran's top sights, is ideally done in the morning when the markets are at their best and the produce is fresh. The walk finishes with a lounge around on the white sand of Pantai Kelan, and you can grab a late lunch from the seafood restaurants. The water here is always inviting for a dip.

START	END	LENGTH
Pasar Desa	Pantai Kelan	2.8km; 2hr

1 A Fruity Start

Jimbaran's **Pasar Desa** (village market, open from 6am to noon) is one of the best markets in Bali for a visit because it's compact, so you can see a lot without wandering forever. There's spices, handicrafts, homewear and souvenirs, but local chefs swear by the quality of the fruit and vegetables here – ever seen a cabbage that big?

2 Holy Rice

Across from the morning market, the ebony-hued **Pura Ulun Siwi** temple dates to the 11th century. It's a snoozy place until it explodes with life for ceremonies and Jl Uluwatu shuts down for processions. The temple is considered one of the most sacred by rice farmers, who travel far to seek blessings here. Its 11-tiered *meru* (multi-roofed shrine) is among Bali's tallest.

3 A Magnificent Beach

Greater than the sum of its parts, white-sand **Pantai Jimbaran** is one of Bali's best beaches. The 4km-long arc of sand is mostly clean, and there is no shortage of places to get a snack, drink, seafood dinner (p77), massage, or to simply laze on a sunlounger or spend hours people-watching. It's also a wonderful place for family swimming; the bay is protected by an unbroken coral reef, which keeps the water calmer than other spots.

4 Something Fishy

Follow the packed white sand north to the beautifully ramshackle **Kedongan Fish Market** (aka Jimbaran Fish Market, open 6am to 5pm). It swings into full gear as just-caught seafood is sold to shoppers and chefs. It's as frenetic as it is fascinating, and the colours, shapes and sizes of the seafood on sale are bewildering. The market is open all day, but it's best in the morning. Don't forget your camera.

5 Hidden Beach Bars

North of the fish market is a string of little-known beach bars strung along a curve of sand (that's not rigorously cleaned) in the shadow of the airport. Most are more no-name than noteworthy, but they offer bargain-priced drinks and fine views from plastic chairs over the bay. **Black Pearl** *(instagram.com/blackpearljimbaranbay)* arranges sunset boat cruises on a fishing boat stocked with coolers of beer.

6 In Plane View

The walk ends on **Pantai Kelan**, where jets roar past, just on the other side of the disconcertingly flimsy picket fence. There are fab views in all directions.

EXPERIENCES

Savour Sunsets & Seafood

SEAFOOD RESTAURANTS

Pantai Jimbaran (MAP: 1 P72 **B4**), one of Bali's best beaches, is also famous for the many seafood restaurants lining its bay. An evening spent here gives you the chance to indulge in freshly caught fish that's carefully barbecued while you soak up the tropical ambience. As evening falls and lights begin to twinkle, aromatic smoke from the grills swirls through the air, and meandering musicians serenade diners.

Along Jimbaran's sweeping 4km beach, there are three groups of restaurants with about 40 eateries in total. The ones on **Pantai Muaya** (MAP: 2 P72 **A6**), in the south, are midrange in terms of pricing and atmosphere. The cluster at **Queen Beach** (MAP: 3 P72 **B4**), the smallest section, is more basic – and cheaper, and better – than the others, although some of the rickety bamboo charm has been lost by new brick façades. **Pantai Kedonganan** (MAP: 4 P72 **B2**), on the fish-market end, is the largest, busiest and pricier section. Sunset is prime time; the restaurants may be almost empty by 8pm.

See Indonesia's Tallest Statue

MONUMENT

MAP: 5 P72 **B6**

One of the first things you'll see as you fly into Bali is the giant Garuda Wisnu Kencana statue inside **GWK Cultural Park** *(gwkbali.com; entry only/incl statue tour 150,000/350,000Rp)*. The sculpture depicts the Hindu god Vishnu riding the mythical bird Garuda. It towers over the Bukit Peninsula and, standing almost 120m high, is among the tallest statues in the world. It was designed by renowned Balinese sculptor Nyoman Nuarta and comprises 3000 tonnes of copper and bronze. It is a feat of art, science and engineering, and it's well worth paying the extra fee for the 45-minute statue tour for the far-reaching views of Bukit. There's also a glass-bottomed walkway and excellent displays sharing details on the design, engineering and construction of the statue. The vast surrounding park has impressive towering limestone cliffs and gardens, a lotus pond, restaurants, kids' activities and a shuttle bus service from the car park.

Soak in Epic Views at Rock Bar

CLIFFSIDE BAR

MAP: 6 P72 **A3**

Perched 14m above the crashing Indian Ocean, the wildly popular **Rock Bar** at the Ayana Resort Bali has a wait to ride the lift down to the bar, sometimes topping one hour. There's a no-backpacks, no-singlets dress code. The food, Med-flavoured bar snacks; the views, spectacular.

Best Places for...

$ Budget $$ Midrange $$$ Top End

Eating

Pantai Muaya Seafood

Kekeluargaan Pandan Sari Cafe $$
7 B6
The beach-end location means less cross-traffic. Skip the indoor tables unless rain looms. *noon-9pm*

Made Bagus Cafe $$
8 B6
Staff here radiate charm. Go for a mixed-seafood platter and ask for extra sauce – it's that good. *8am-9pm*

Queen Beach Seafood

Warung Ramayana $$
9 B4
Fishing boats dot the beach in front of this long-running favourite. The seafood marinates from early morning, and the grills smoke all evening. *9am-10pm*

Warung Bamboo $$
10 B4
Slightly more appealing than its neighbours, though all have a raffish charm. Choose your own seafood; sides and sauces included. *10am-11pm*

Pantai Kedonganan Seafood

Warung Made $
11 B1
Buy a fish in the market and get it grilled at this rustic stall near the market entrance (sides included). *7am-6pm*

Jimbaran Bay Seafood $$
12 B2
Especially welcoming, with a huge variety of tables inside, on the terrace and out where your toes tickle the sand. *10am-10pm*

Cuisine Cafe $$
13 C2
More stylish than many of its competitors. Mod lights and nautical clichés offer atmosphere inside. *9am-10pm*

More than Seafood

Cuca Restaurant $$
14 C4
Not a smouldering coconut husk in sight at this top tapas bistro serving Spanish favourites. *noon-11pm*

Warung Nasi Bali Kedonganan $
15 D3
Indonesian comfort food is the order of the day at this no-frills warung (food stall). The nasi goreng draws fans. *8am-11pm*

Bull's Coffee Jimbaran $
16 B6
Sources excellent local beans and sells brews at affordable prices. Good bagels, pastries and sandwiches. *8am-10pm*

Drinking

Drinks with a View

Black Pearl
17 A1
Best of the beach-shack bars along Pantai Kelan. Stiff drinks served with a pirate's flair. Its sunset cruises are a hoot. *4-10pm*

Jimbaran Beach Club
18 A6
Chilled beach bar at Jimbaran's posh end, with no pool but a big ocean to swim in, plus comfy loungers. *8am-11pm*

See p89 for eating, drinking and shopping listings

Researched by Jade Bremner

Explore Uluwatu & Around

It's hard to imagine that the dry Bukit Peninsula was almost uninhabited. Once it was only known for its impressive temple, Pura Luhur Uluwatu, dating to the 11th century. In the five decades since the epic wave at Uluwatu was first ridden, the ululating sound of its name has echoed around the world among board riders. After the surfers came the luxury lodgings, buzzing cafes, restaurants, and a steady flow of both health-conscious travellers and a party crowd. Find early-morning yoga sessions and rejuvenating massage houses or sip drinks all day in the clifftop beach clubs if you choose. For many, Uluwatu and the areas around it are more a life choice than a holiday.

Getting Around

Taxis

The traffic is bad, even by Bali's low standards. Narrow streets abound along the main road to Uluwatu, where there are constant engine sounds. The good news? Taxis are plentiful via Gojek and Grab, but leave extra time to get to your destination.

Walking & Motorbikes

Walking is perilous as there are few footpaths around the Bukit Peninsula. Many choose to book a motorbike on Grab or Gojek, which dodge some of the traffic, but the weaving can be nerve-jangling as a passenger. Watch out for cops levying fines for lack of helmets.

THE BEST

SUNSET EXPERIENCE
Pura Luhur Uluwatu (p82)

BEACH ESCAPE
Dreamland Beach (p87)

WAVES FOR SURFING
Pantai Suluban (p84)

BEACH CLUB
El Kabron (p88)

WELLNESS
Istana (p88)

Dreamland Beach (p87)
WONDERFULNATURE/SHUTTERSTOCK

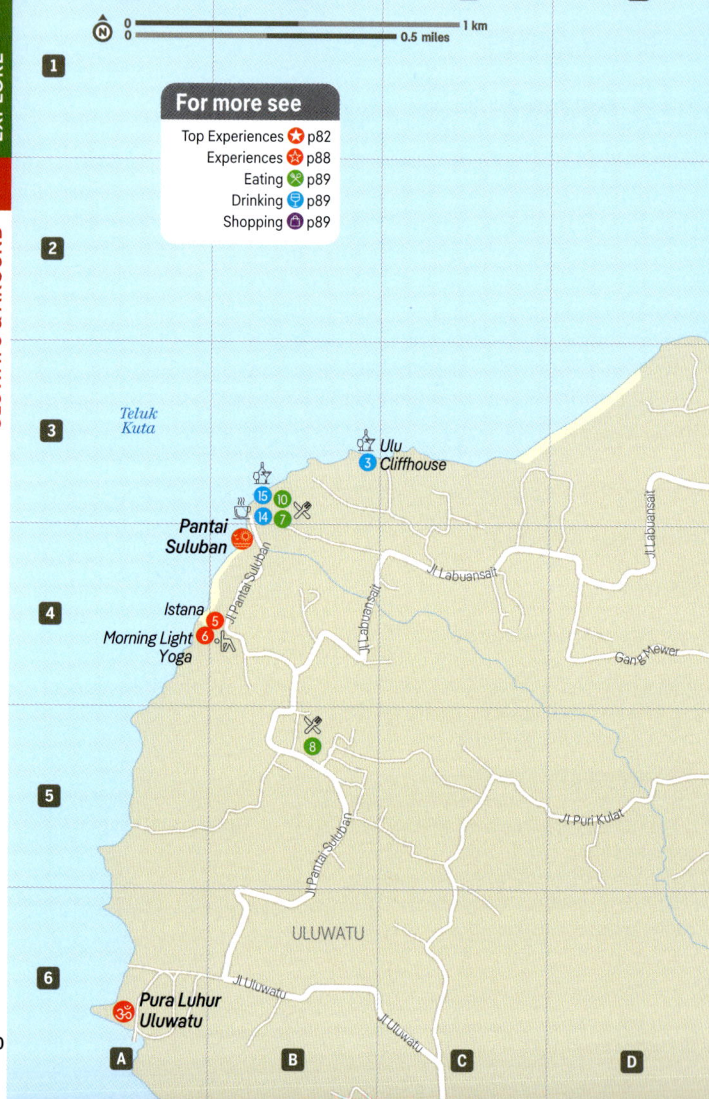
A
B
C
D
0
1 km
0
0.5 miles
1
2
3
4
5
6
For more see
Top Experiences p82
Experiences p88
Eating p89
Drinking p89
Shopping p89
Teluk Kuta
Ulu
3 Cliffhouse
15
10
14
7
Pantai Suluban
Jl Pantai Suluban
Jl Labuansait
Jl Labuansait
Jl Labuansait
Istana
5
Morning Light
6
Yoga
Gang Mewer
8
Jl Puri Kulat
Jl Pantai Suluban
ULUWATU
Jl Uluwatu
Jl Uluwatu
Pura Luhur Uluwatu
A
B
C
D

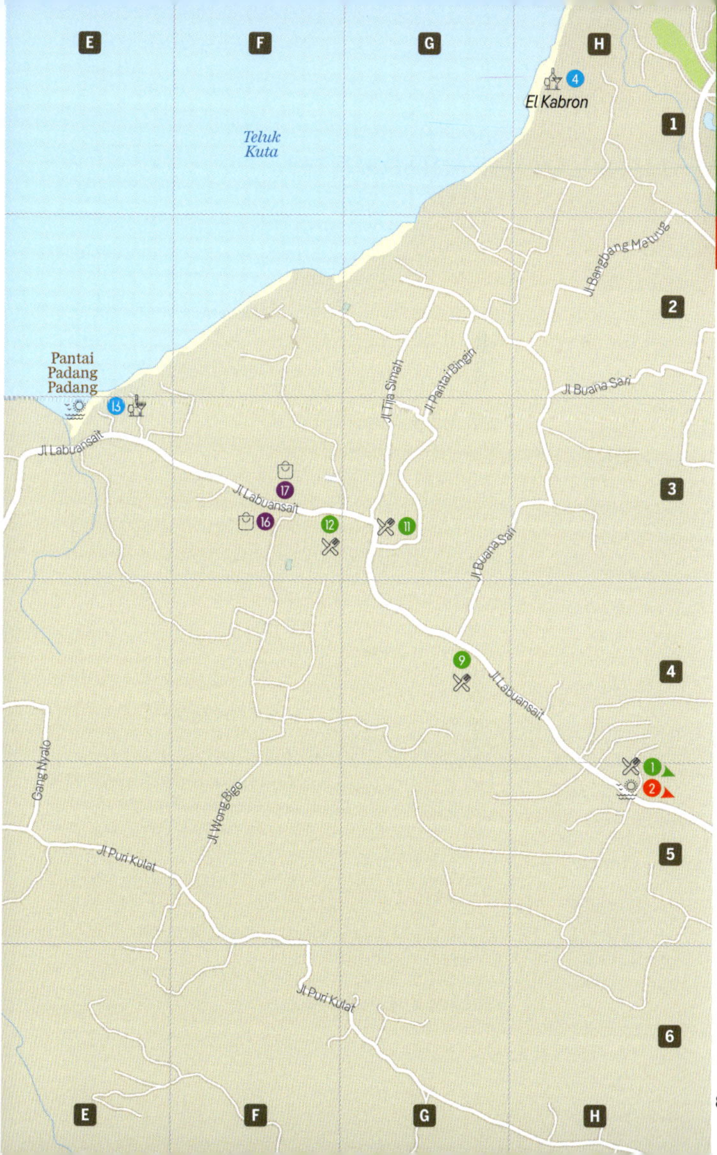

E
F
G
H
El Kabron
4
Teluk Kuta
1
Jl Bangbang Matuug
2
Pantai Padang Padang
13
Jl Labuansait
Jl Tija Simah
Jl Pantai Bingin
Jl Buana Sari
3
17
16
Jl Labuansait
12
11
Jl Buana Sari
9
4
Jl Labuansait
1
2
Gang Nyalo
Jl Wong Bigo
Jl Puri Kulat
5
Jl Puri Kulat
6
E
F
G
H

★ TOP EXPERIENCE

Pura Luhur Uluwatu

According to ancient Balinese scripts, Pura Luhur Uluwatu *(uluwatutemple.id; adult/child 50,000/30,000Rp)* is a magical portal that can transport those who set eyes on it directly to heaven. It is spectacular, and even the casual observer can feel its significance. Sunset dance performances add to the magic.

MAP P80 **A6**

PLANNING TIP
Beware of the temple's monkeys – when not energetically fornicating, they're snatching sunglasses, phones and everything else. Ask around at the gate to hire a guide who's good at shooing them away.

Scan this QR code to book tickets for Kecak performances and avoid the queues.

Sacred & Beautiful

The landscape, sculpted gardens and dramatic, 70m-high cliffs rising from the Indian Ocean amount to what would be a highly spiritual spot, even without the presence of one of Bali's most important sea temples. The temple was built in the 11th century and is believed to be one of the most spiritually charged sites in Bali, although the crowds can disturb this place of worship. Come early in the day to avoid them, and take time to walk along the clifftop path for gorgeous views of the temple and the rolling swells below.

Sea Temple Protections

The legendary 16th-century priest Nirartha, who finished his life here, is credited with introducing many of the complexities of Balinese Hinduism to the island, as well as establishing the chain of *pura segara* (sea temples). These sacred coastal spots honour the sea gods and protect Bali from sea demons. Each temple was intended to be within sight of the next.

Sunset Kecak Dance

As the sun slips below the Indian Ocean, the air around Pura Luhur Uluwatu reverberates with

MITCHELL SOEHARSONO/SHUTTERSTOCK

the hypnotising '*chak-chak-chak*' chant as Kecak (pronounced ke-chak) performers mesmerise the audience gathered to watch what has become an iconic display of Balinese culture. With the majestic Uluwatu cliffs as a backdrop, the dancers enact tales from the Ramayana (one of the great holy books of Hinduism). The dancers' traditional attire, the flickering flames, and the rhythmic sounds and movements create a true spectacle. While the Kecak dance is performed in various locations around the island, including Ubud (p115), the one in Uluwatu is the most popular.

Be prepared to sit in unholy traffic jams on the way there (or sidestep them with a motorbike), and aim to arrive at least an hour before the show starts.

QUICK BREAK
The many excellent Uluwatu cafes and eateries are easily reached in under 15 minutes by car or motorbike; otherwise, there are simple refreshments available outside the temple entrance.

★ TOP EXPERIENCE

Pantai Suluban

With its consistent waves, Uluwatu is one of the world's best places to surf. The five peaks at Pantai Suluban are affectionately referred to as the 'Ulus'. These bucket-list breaks were immortalised in the 1970s surf film, *Morning of the Earth.*

MAP P80 **B4**

PLANNING TIP
The cliffs above Pantai Suluban provide exceptional views for observing the action – it's hard to beat the view from **Single Fin** *(singlefinbali.com)* and the cluster of cliffside cafes here.

Scan this QR code for info on the Bukit's surf breaks.

Racetracks

None of Uluwatu's breaks are suitable for beginners. If you're an experienced surfer, then paddle out from the famous cave at Pantai Suluban – the entry point to the Ulus – to reach **Racetracks**. This is the fastest section, with the steepest walls and the roundest barrels; at mid- to lower tides you'll have access to some of the world's most perfect tubes.

Peak & Outside Corner

Just south of the cave is the **Peak**. It's not for the faint-hearted, and is best avoided around low tide, when it can be uncomfortably shallow.

Outside Corner, where the swell can rise to triple overhead, is where the 'Balinese Pipeline' starts to work big-wave magic. It breaks beyond the Peak and fires right across the line of Racetracks.

Bombie & Temples

South of Outside Corner (and breaking even further out) is the **Bombie**, which can reach 40ft and should be avoided unless you're a big-wave charger of note. If you're looking for a quiet wave, then head for **Temples**, a relatively fickle spot south of the Peak that can break on smaller days; the longer paddle also helps to keep crowds to a minimum.

★ TOP EXPERIENCE

Paragliding the Coast

You don't need a drone to see Uluwatu's coastline from above; you can fly like a bird with a parachute after a thrilling launch off the cliff over Gunung Payung beach. Taking a tandem flight along the coastline is an exhilarating experience.

Taking Flight

Launch sites dot the clifftops above the secluded, usually empty **Gunung Payung** beach. After being given a number, passengers are directed to the paraglider, which has a comfy chair for two. Choose either a 15-minute or half-hour flight and swoop along the coastline, offering bird's-eye perspectives of reefs, golden sandy coves, and the nearby **Pura Dhang Kahyangan Gunung Payung** temple. Each flight includes the option to hold an action camera and keep the videos as part of the experience price (make sure your phone has 6GB of space to hold the photos). For extra thrills, ask your instructor to dip and swoop below and above the cliffs.

Secret Beach Visit

After your flight, explore the idyllic Gunung Payung beach, a well-kept secret on Bali's south coast. To get to the beach you have to walk through an ancient amphitheatre before descending steep steps to the pristine sandy shore. On the beach there's a small snack shop plus kayak rental. At low tide, explore the natural caves at the beach's western end.

PLANNING TIP

Bring all the beach gear you want when visiting Gunung Payung beach – there's a beach shuttle service from the car park above *(return 25,000Rp)* for those who prefer not to walk down and up.

Scan this QR code to book a flight with Bali Paragliding Tours.

Drive Uluwatu

The Bukit Peninsula's coastline is dotted with idyllic white-sand beaches backed by striking limestone cliffs. Trying to walk between the beaches is perilous owing to the narrow, traffic-choked roads and lack of footpaths; instead take a motorbike to hop between these top beaches.

START	END	LENGTH
Pantai Balangan	Pantai Suluban	12.5km; 3hr

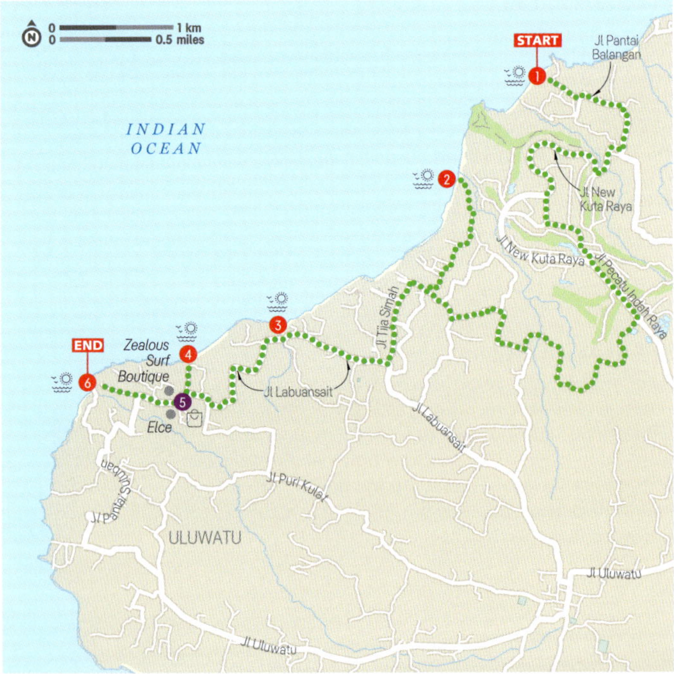

INDIAN OCEAN
0 1 km
0 0.5 miles
START
END
Jl Pantai Balangan
Jl New Kuta Raya
Jl Pecatu Indah Raya
Jl Tija Simah
Jl Labuansait
Zealous Surf Boutique
Elce
Jl Pantai Suluban
Jl Puri Kulat
ULUWATU
Jl Uluwatu

1 Charm of Balangan

Somehow, **Pantai Balangan** has resisted the development that has altered the charm of neighbouring beaches like Dreamland. The long strip of sweet white sand, backed by a ragtag collection of rickety bamboo cafes, survives (you can park near the sand), and the stunning views across the indigo surf are as good as ever. Take the meandering 4km Jl New Kuta Raya road to Dreamland Beach.

2 Rocky Shores & White Sands

Backed by cliffs, lively and incredibly photogenic **Dreamland Beach** is a 400m-long sandy stretch with turquoise waters, pulling crowds of both tourists and expats (in fact everyone...and their dogs). There's even more of a show when the surf's big.

3 The Hollywood Beach

Following Jl Labuansait, you reach the entry point to pint-sized **Pantai Padang Padang** – popular since it starred in the 2010 romantic drama film *Eat Pray Love*. Today, the white-sand cove at the end of the concrete steps, just off Labuansait, draws surfers and loungers. You'll have to come early to snare a rental recliner and umbrella. Hit the stalls down on the sand for refreshments.

4 Hidden by Height

Continue on Jl Labuansait until you come to the 130 steep steps leading down the limestone cliff-face to serene **Thomas Beach**. The beach feels quite secluded, as lush vegetation shrouds its steep sides. There are some warungs (food stalls) here, and you can swim or surf the smaller, beginner waves.

5 Pause to Shop

Browse the cluster of shops and cafes at the bend in Jl Labuansait. If you have time, pop into **Elce**, which sells Bali-made beachwear, and there's also **Zealous Surf Boutique**, with clothes made by and for women, for everything you'll need on the waves.

6 Bali's Best Ocean Views

Pantai Suluban is renowned as the entry point to the famous 'Ulus' surf breaks (p84). But from the top it also has some of the best ocean views in Bali, including those from Single Fin (p89). After weaving past cliffside cafes, you'll emerge into a limestone cove. At low tide, you can access a small 'hidden beach' through the cave.

EXPERIENCES

Explore Beautiful Beaches BEACH VENUES

White-sand beaches dot the south coast of Bali. The entire region is a bit of a building site, but amenities – and selfies – abound, as these beaches are major day-trip destinations, and, unlike other beaches, are easily reached by roads or elevators.

For one of the best, try **Sundays Beach Club** (MAP: 1 P80 **H5**; *sundays beachclub.com; 450,000Rp*), a beach venue with a good restaurant; the entry fee includes 250,000Rp food credit to spend here. Stand-up paddleboards, kayaks and snorkelling gear are available, while evenings bring beach bonfires. Nearby is popular **Pantai Melasti** (MAP: 2 P80 **H5**), with its many lively beach clubs. A reef forms natural pools at low tide, and there's a sunset Kecak performance (p82).

Experience Beach Club Life SUNSET PARTIES

Uluwatu's party scene is different from Bali's other late-night coastal spots; it's more laid-back, with a focus on day drinking at relaxed but exclusive beach clubs, usually attached to upmarket or boutique hotels. Here, a slightly older crowd relaxes with plush daybeds and infinity pools in stylish spaces, typically with dramatic clifftop views. Instead of clubwear, patrons don bikinis or long shorts, and the energy and music build through the afternoon, with creative cocktails flowing and international DJs spinning, up to a climax at sunset. **Ulu Cliffhouse** (MAP: 3 P80 **B3**; *uluclifffhouse.com; free entry*) hosts parties over Dreamland Beach with rotating DJs, and **El Kabron** (MAP: 4 P80 **H1**; *elkabron.com; minimum spend per person 400,000Rp*) is one of the Bukit's coolest places to revel, perched on the clifftop over Bingin. It runs a Hedonist Sunset Party twice a week as well as themed pool parties.

Stretch with a View YOGA STUDIOS

This region rivals Canggu and Ubud for its yoga offerings and wellness treatments. Doing your moves on a mat overlooking the expanse of the Indian Ocean is a fine way to start the day.

The **Istana** (MAP: 5 P80 **B4**; *theistana.com; spa sessions from 200,000Rp*) is a luxurious clifftop retreat overlooking the Ulus (p84). This meditation resort hosts two yoga classes a day and drop-ins are welcome. Nearby, **Morning Light Yoga** (MAP: 6 P80 **A4**; *uluwatusurf villas.com; per session 150,000Rp*) has daily morning classes in a beautiful grass-roofed yoga space surrounded by lush tropical beauty and ocean views.

Best Places for...

$ Budget $$ Midrange $$$ Top End

See p80 for map of locations

Eating

Atmospheric Eats

By the Cliff $$

Popular post-surf spot with a board rack and healthy eats, from acai bowls and avo-on-toast brekkies to good salads. *8am-8pm*

Mellow Meals

Land's End Café $$

8 B5

This daytime cafe has a good selection of smoothies, smoothie bowls and breakfasts, with vegan options. *8am-3.30pm*

Warung Local $

9 G4

Popular local-style eatery with an array of Indonesian dishes. A great budget option; tasty lunch buffet. *8am-10pm*

Jeffry Warung $

Right at the surf point, this is a low-key choice for serious surfers. Sandwiches and Indo classics for cheap. *7am-7pm*

Alchemy Uluwatu $$

Nourish your body at Alchemy's plant-based restaurant with heaped salads and delicious desserts. *7.30am-10pm*

Bukit Cafe $$

12 F3

Heaping plates of Australian-style brunch composed of fresh, local ingredients. Think smoothie bowls, smashed avocado and live music in the evenings. *8am-10pm*

Drinking

Drinks with a View

Dugong Lounge & Bar

Gaze over the curved infinity pool to the Indian Ocean while enjoying the wines, cocktails and juices here. *8am-11pm*

La Terrazza

Drinks and Italian bites on the cliff at Uluwatu. Book a seat to nab one of the Bukit's best sunset views. *8am-9pm*

Single Fin

Famous bar on the cliffs overlooking the Ulus. Great spot for sunset drinks; Sunday nights are a scene. *8am-10pm*

Shopping

Uluwatu Boutiques

Uma and Leopold

16 F3

Flowing dresses, light playsuits and lots of linen, this Brazilian womenswear brand uses Balinese-inspired craft and design. *9am-9pm*

By the Sea Uluwatu

17 F3

Upmarket resort wear with low-impact materials including linens, breathable cottons and high-grade rayon. *10am-9pm*

See p97
for eating
listings

Researched by
Jade Bremner

Explore
Nusa Dua & Around

The exclusive resort enclave of Nusa Dua, with its manicured lawns, pristine beach and luxury hotels, flanks the northeastern peninsula of the Bukit. Its own little peninsula, Nusa Gede Island (sometimes called Peninsula Island), which has been tamed into a park called the Garden of Hope, is fringed by dramatically ragged limestone edges that are in stark contrast to its manicured surroundings.

Created in the 1970s, the area was designed to compete with international beach resorts. Balinese culture takes the form of slightly condensed cultural displays, and high-end resort restaurants serve 'local' cuisine, often with hefty tabs.

Getting Around

Walking & Cycling

Once in the area, you can stroll the long beach promenade and enjoy the views. It's also possible to rent bikes to get around and cover more distance quickly along the promenade.

Taxis

Many non-resort restaurants provide transport from Nusa Dua and Tanjung Benoa hotels, and taxis, as well as Grab and Gojek rides, are easily had. Nusa Dua's wide, landscaped boulevards are rarely clogged, but the same can't be said for the roads outside the gates.

THE BEST

BEACH
Pantai Geger (p96)

FINE ART
Museum Pasifika (p93)

NATURAL SITE
Water blow (p94)

WATER SPORTS
Dogol Surf Lesson (p96)

BEACH EATS
Le Bleu by K Club (p97)

Pantai Geger (p96)
URANG SANGKA/SHUTTERSTOCK

A
B
C
D
1
2
3
4
5
6
See Enlargement
BENOA
200 m
0.1 miles
Selat Badung
Jl Segara Lor
6
Masjid Jami'Mujahidin
5
Caow Eng Bio
4
Pura Dalem Ning
17
Jl Segara Geni
Jl Pratama
Teluk Benoa
16
Bumbu Bali Cooking School
1
Jl Tol Bali Mandara
Sri Lanka Beach
Jl Ngurah Rai Bypass
Jl Pratama Raya
12
NUSA DUA
13
15
10
Jl Nusa Dua
Museum Pasifika
BUALU
8
Jl Srikandi
Jl Raya Bvalu Ungasan
Jl Pantai Mengiat
14
3
Dogol Surf Lesson
7
Jl Terompong
Golf Course
11
2
Pantai Geger
18
Jl Pura Gegar
Jl Nusa Dua Selatan
9
1 km
0.5 miles
For more see
Top Experience p93
Experiences p96
Eating p97

★ TOP EXPERIENCE

Museum Pasifika

Museum Pasifika's impressive collection spans 11 rooms and more than 600 paintings, sculptures and artefacts by Indonesian, Pacific Ocean and European artists. Leave a couple of hours to wander these great works.

Indonesian Masters

Dive into the nation's cultural richness by viewing works by more than 50 Indonesian Masters, including Romantic painter Raden Saleh, Balinese stone sculptor and painter Lempad, expressionist Affandi, plus colourful but poignant modern and contemporary painters Hendra and Kobot.

Pacific Room

The Michoutouchkine and Pilioko collection is terrific and bound to appeal to children, with dynamic displays of around 200 sculptures and tapa (bark cloth), from warrior apparel and striking ritual masks to carvings from 10 different Pacific nations. Don't miss the tikis and textiles.

Indo-European Artists

Artists from Europe who lived and worked in Indonesia are also on display, including pieces by Arie Smit, Theo Meier and Adrien-Jean Le Mayeur de Merpres, plus pieces by French artists Matisse and Gauguin.

Activities

You can book ahead to participate in many artistic activities at the museum, such as canvas painting and Balinese dance.

MAP P92 **C4**

PLANNING TIP
The QR code displayed at the museum allows you to download a free audio guide for more information about the artworks on display.

Scan this QR code to reserve tickets in advance at a discounted price.

WALKING TOUR

Walk Nusa Dua

Nusa Dua means 'two islands', and this walk takes in both. These oases of green, with manicured lawns, natural rock features and spectacular blowholes, are nestled amid turquoise waters with beach and ocean views. You'll find peaceful places along the route to pause for a while (or a whole afternoon).

START	END	LENGTH
Museum Pasifika	Water blow	1.8km; 2hr

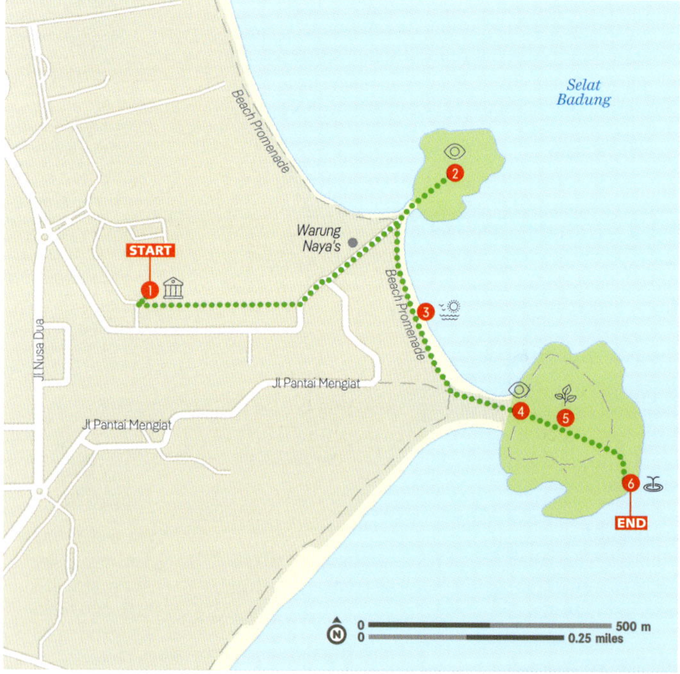

1 Art to Start

Start at the **Museum Pasifika** (p93) for a dose of culture amid manicured Nusa Dua gardens. Afterwards walk due east, then northeast, along a pleasant tree-shaded lane that passes a row of casual (and very good) cafes serving classic Indonesian fare. Warung Naya's (p97) comes especially recommended.

2 Island One

Directly ahead is the first of Nusa Dua's two lovely islands. Walk along the isthmus path between the two calm, curving crescent beaches to **Nusa Dharma**, a small dome of an islet with large expanses of grass, and the small temple of Pura Nusa Dharma. The views back west will give some idea of the scope of the resort enclave.

3 Surf Beach

Return to the isthmus and walk south on the **Beach Promenade** along the frequently raked sands of **Pantai Nusa Dua**. If you fancy a cool-off, the water-sports vendors here offer rental surfboards and stand-up paddleboards (SUPs) at prices well below those of the resorts. Surfers, FYI: during the wet season (October to March), the reef offshore has consistent swells. The main break is 1km off the beach to the south.

4 Island Two

Next up is **Nusa Gede** (aka Peninsula Island). It's larger than Nusa Dharma and has become a special events venue for concerts aimed at boosting Nusa Dua's appeal with Gen Z. It's a green oasis, with well-preserved flora and some beautiful views of the coastline and Nusa Penida.

5 Artworks & Serenity

The beautifully serene **Garden of Hope** is fringed by dramatically ragged limestone edges that are in stark contrast to the manicured surroundings. Carved stones bear inspirational quotes, and there are plenty of statues and other public art to enjoy. It's also a good spot for a picnic (or a nap).

6 There They Blow

The natural phenomenon of **water blow** *(25,000Rp)* is where powerful waves crash against a slab of dangerously jagged rocks, and the water is forced up through steep, tight gaps in the limestone, creating dramatic water eruptions up to 10m high. For years, this natural phenomenon was obscured by vegetation and the jagged limestone made it difficult (and dangerous) to get closer for a good view. For safety, a concrete walkway and viewing points have now been built, and the path will take you safely over the rocks and close to the blowholes.

EXPERIENCES

Learn to Cook a Balinese Meal
COOKERY SCHOOL

MAP: 1 P92 **B2**

The much-lauded **Bumbu Bali Cooking School** *(artcafebumbubali.com; classes from 1,250,000Rp)* at the eponymous restaurant strives to get to the roots of Balinese cooking. Courses start with an introduction to Balinese flavours by chef, author and owner Heinz von Holzen, assisted by his resident experts. They detail the importance of aromatic spices such as ginger, turmeric, lemongrass and galangal before the class prepares 12 iconic dishes. Students (a maximum of eight in total) then feast on their work for lunch. Booking in advance is advised. The restaurant is one of the Bukit's best.

Surf, Dive & Have Watery Thrills
WATER SPORTS

Surfers will find breaks to suit all abilities in the area, including Nikko (a fast right-hand wave) in front of Hilton Bali Resort; Geger Right and Left at **Pantai Geger** (MAP: 2 P92 **B5**); plus advanced spots Chicken Wings and Mushroom Rock. **Dogol Surf Lesson** (MAP: 3 P92 **C4**; *instagram.com/surf_lessondogol; surf rental from 180,000Rp*) will hook you up with a board; the beach shack is just before the entrance of Nusa Gede Island (p95). Tanjung Benoa to the north also offers a variety of aquatic thrills. All the centres feature parasailing or banana-boat rides – check equipment and safety credentials with operators before signing up. **BMR Dive & Water Sports** *(bmrbaliofficial.com; from 338,000Rp)* is an established operator offering activities including flyboarding, scuba diving, snorkelling, parasailing, jet skiing and banana-boat rides. All can be booked online.

Experience Indonesian Religious Culture
RELIGIOUS SITES

For a dive into Indonesia's religious culture, head north to the village of Benoa, around 6km north of Nusa Dua beach, at the tip of the Tanjung Benoa peninsula. The founding principle of Indonesia is Pancasila, a core philosophical theory of unity that holds a belief in God without predominance of one specific religion – an important tenet in a nation with myriad faiths, including six that are officially recognised. Here, within 200m of each other, are three places of worship of different faiths and architectural styles: **Pura Dalem Ning** (MAP: 4 P92 **D1**), a Balinese Hindu temple with a soaring triple entrance; **Caow Eng Bio** (MAP: 5 P92 **D1**), a brightly coloured Chinese Buddhist temple with traditional archways; and **Masjid Jami'Mujahidin** (MAP: 6 P92 **C1**), a domed mosque.

Best Places for...

$ Budget $$ Midrange $$$ Top End

See p92 for map of locations

Eating

Asian & Balinese Meals

Art Cafe Bumbu Bali $$
7 B5
A bright, airy Nusa Dua extension of the long-running Bumbu Bali Cooking School, serving top local fare. *9am-10pm*

Warung Dobiel $
8 B4
This is a good stop for *babi guling* (spit-roasted pork). It's a no-frills experience, with stools and shared tables. *10am-4pm*

Koral Restaurant $$$

9 B6
The architecturally stunning Apurva Kempinski Bali is Bali's first aquarium restaurant. *noon-3pm & 5.30-10.30pm*

Beachside Dining

Le Bleu by K Club $$$
10 C4
Chic spot on Nusa Dua Beach with an impressive raised woven roof, chilled beats and fine international cuisine. *10am-11pm*

Kayuputi $$$
11 B5
Beachside dining at a ridiculously lavish restaurant in the St Regis Bali. Fresh seafood, delicate desserts and culinary classics. *noon-10pm*

Hotel Dining

Udupi $$
12 B3
Stylish Indian restaurant in a midrange hotel, the Bali Sunshine Inn, with an emphasis on vegetarian dishes. *8am-10pm*

Arwana $$$

13 C4
Seafood brunch is hugely popular at this spot on the Laguna resort's beach promenade. *11am-10pm*

Pasar Senggol $$$
14 C4
A romantic, torchlight Indonesian buffet served nightly in the Grand Hyatt Bali, accompanied by a Balinese dance performance. Ask for spice 'Bali-style'. *6-10pm*

Low-Cost Meals

Warung Naya's $
15 C4
One of several unassuming Indonesian cafes near Nusa Dharma; has shady tables good for people-watching. Tasty, classic fare. *8am-8pm*

Atlichnaya $

16 B2
Lively, cheerful cafe/bar with three locations around Tanjung Benoa. Cocktails, and Western and local fare at a fraction of resort prices. *3-11pm*

Casual Seafood

Surya Cafe $
17 C1
A bare-bones seafood grill at Tanjung Benoa's northern tip. Everything's fresh; ask for extra *bawang putih* (garlic). *noon-9pm*

Nusa Dua Beach Grill $$
18 B6
A good spot for day-trippers, beyond the Mulia resort on Pantai Geger. Good drinks menu, fresh seafood and sea views. *8.30am-10pm*

See p105
for eating and
drinking listings

Researched by Jade Bremner

Explore Sanur

Sanur's waterfront promenade is noticeably laid-back compared to the beachfront bustle of Bali's southwest beaches, and draws a different crowd. Families and older travellers tend to prefer the luxury resorts or humble homestays here to Uluwatu's party vibes. A peaceful, shaded walkway connects several kilometres of relaxed bars, restaurants, shops and hotels.

The area's refreshingly verdant and spacious resorts offer tropical gardens, big communal pools and lots of facilities. Off the beach the ocean is protected by a reef, with waves breaking around half a kilometre out, meaning calm waters for swimming and mellow water sports. Traditional daily life is still evident in the villagers who harvest seafood from the reefs and in the traditional colourful *jukung* (outrigger fishing boats).

Getting Around

Taxi

Sanur borders Denpasar, and the capital is just a short drive away, while Ubud is conveniently north. For trips to/from the airport, use the toll road as the Ngurah Rai Bypass running past Sanur often gets jammed. Ride apps make getting around town easy.

Walking & Cycling

The beachfront walkway is a 5km, often-shaded pathway you can walk or cycle (bikes for rent along the route) for a scenic car-free way to enjoy Sanur. The busy Jl Danau Tamblingan strip is the commercial spine of Sanur and parallels the beach; pavements mean it can be explored by foot.

THE BEST

NIGHT MARKET
Pasar Sindhu (p104)

DAYTIME DELIGHT
Sanur Beachfront Promenade (p104)

KAYAKING
Sanur Beach (p104)

SEASONAL EVENT
Bali Kite Festival (p104)

SURFING
Rip Curl School of Surf (p104)

Bali Kite Festival (p104)
RIDO ZAEN/SHUTTERSTOCK

Jl Hang Tuah
Denpasar (5km)
Jl Ngurah Rai Bypass
Jl Danau Bratan
Jl Danau Buyan
Jl Segara Ayu
Jl Danau Tondano
Jl Pantai Sindhu
Sindhu Night Market
Jl Danau Tamblingan
Beachfront Walk
Nusa Lembongan (20km)
Selat Badung
Jl Pantai Karang
Sanur Beachfront Promenade
Jl Tirtanadi
Sanur Beach
Jl Duyung
Jl Danau Poso
SANUR
Jl Kesumasari
Jl Cemara
Rip Curl School of Surf
500 m
0.25 miles
For more see
Top Experience p101
Experiences p104
Eating p105
Drinking p105

★ TOP EXPERIENCE

Trip to Nusa Lembongan

Sanur is often visited as a jumping-off point to Bali's western islands, easily reachable in 40 minutes from Bali by fast boat. Make the detour for a sleepy place rich with Hindu culture and dramatic cliffs pounded by waves, plus quiet mangrove forests.

Underwater World

Nusa Lembongan falls within the Coral Triangle, a marine region revered for its exceptional biodiversity, and the diving and snorkelling here are sublime. You'll likely see schools of colourful reef fish, curious turtles and majestic manta rays gliding with the currents. Between July and October, it's also possible to spot huge *Mola mola* here. **Bali Hai** *(balihaicruises.com, 2 dives incl equipment from 1,800,000Rp)* is recommended for dive trips.

Surf Uncrowded Waves

Spectacular Pantai Jungutbatu, a 2km-long stretch of Lembongan's coast, has three offshore reefs that catch consistent surf daily – on rare occasions, you'll even see barrelling overhead waves. **Playgrounds** is the southernmost and easiest-to-reach surf spot, accessible from Song Lambung Beach. Board rental is available for 150,000Rp per hour.

Mangrove Kayaking

The northeastern corner of Lembongan is wrapped in an immense tangle of mangroves. Shady tunnels wind through trees – the world here feels quiet, still and cool. Hire a **local boatman** *(30min 150,000Rp)* to pole you through the waterways, rent a kayak and explore on your own, or take a **guided kayak tour** *(1hr 175,000Rp)*.

PLANNING TIP
Pack light and be prepared to get wet stepping off the boat at the island. Boats moor off the beach at Nusa Lembongan, necessitating a wade through the shallows with luggage.

Scan this QR code to book a fast ferry to Nusa Lembongan.

WALKING TOUR

Walk Sanur

The Sanur Beachfront Promenade has been delighting residents and visitors for decades. More than 5km long, it curves past resorts, cafes, temples, fishing boats, vendors and elegant villas. While you stroll, look out across the water to the island of Nusa Penida. The promenade is also good for cycling (p104).

START	END	LENGTH
Warung Mak Beng	Mertasari Beach	5km; 3hr

1 Legendary Meal

Where Jl Hang Tuah dead-ends at the sea, you'll find the ever-popular favourite **Warung Mak Beng** (p105). Stop here for a fortifying meal of *ikan laut goreng* (barbecued fish).

2 Artful Beginning

Head south on the beachfront walkway. You'll soon reach the walled compound of **Museum Le Mayeur**, the former home of Belgian artist Adrien-Jean Le Mayeur. Inside a museum houses 90 of his paintings; although closed for refurbishment on our last visit, the wonderful Balinese-style architecture can be viewed from the promenade.

3 A Medical Miracle

Further down the promenade, you'll reach the high-rise **Bali Beach Hotel**. Built in 1965 to kickstart international tourism, the hotel horrified the Balinese, who quickly passed a rule that no building in the area could be higher than a coconut palm. The ageing hotel was on life support until thrown a lifeline with the advent of the Bali International Hospital.

4 New & Old at Tandjung Sari Hotel

You'll soon encounter another radical change to Sanur: the massive **Icon Bali Mall**, drawing shoppers in beachwear from its entrance right off the beach to designer shops, from Calvin Klein to Ted Baker. Just a bit further along is the **Tandjung Sari Hotel**, built in the 1960s by local artists to become a model for hotels island-wide.

5 Top Temple

Further along is one of several temples lining the beach: **Pura Tandjung Sari** has the classic carved *candi bentar* (split gateway). Note the wealth of detail.

6 Pit Stop

Seagrass by the Beach is a good spot to stop for a fresh coconut juice or fragrant Indonesian curry, with a view of both the promenade and beach for people-watching.

7 Local Life

Continuing south, look for the multihued *jukung*, **traditional fishing boats**, pulled ashore under the trees. Notice the painted faces on the front. Also, keep an eye out for the turtle tanks near Jl Kusumasari, where there are young hatchlings and displays on Bali's endangered sea turtles.

8 Fun in the Sun

As you approach **Pantai Mertisari**, the beach becomes the domain of residents who come here for a swim and a stroll along the breakwater. Simple warungs (food stalls) sell refreshments. The Bali Kite Festival (p104) takes place near here, usually on a windy day in July or August

EXPERIENCES

Sample Street Food at a Night Market FOOD MARKET

MAP: 1 P100 **B2**

Sanur's atmospheric **Pasar Sindhu** might at first glance appear small, but its food stalls are a hive of activity in the evening and offer a fantastic opportunity to sample a wide variety of tasty traditional Indonesian fare from around 25,000Rp a dish. Many stalls are retro and very photogenic in appearance. Each specialises in something different, and most of the food is prepared while you wait.

Surf or Paddle Sanur's Barrier Reef WATER SPORTS

Sanur's tranquil coastline is protected by a barrier reef that stretches for 7km and creates a series of waveless beaches – a real novelty on Bali's south-facing coastline. The crystal-clear water at **Sanur Beach** (MAP: 2 P100 **C5**) rarely goes past waist-level, making it ideal for kayaking and stand-up paddleboarding *(rentals 100,000Rp)*. Surfers will have a long paddle of up to 1km to reach the waves, but schools along the beach, including **Rip Curl School of Surf** (MAP: 3 P100 **A6**; *ripcurlschoolofsurf.com; 2hr lessons 850,000Rp*), offer boat rides with boards and lessons, complete with insurance (a rarity in Bali).

Cycle the Coastline CYCLING

MAP: 4 P100 **C4**

The paved, almost-6km-long **Sanur Beachfront Promenade** is perfect for a leisurely cycle exploring the coastline of one of Bali's most family-friendly beach towns. There are comfortable cruisers and kids' bikes available for rent *(1hr 20,000Rp)* along the promenade, long stretches of which have dedicated bike lanes. You'll find plenty of places along the way to stop for coffee, food, shopping or a massage.

Experience the Bali Kite Festival FESTIVAL

MAP: 5 P100 **B1**

During the windy season, Bali's sky is dominated by huge kites flown as a thanksgiving message to the gods for abundant harvests. At Sanur, the hub of the **Bali Kite Festival**, teams compete to get the most spectacular kites soaring on the thermals. This colourful festival is usually held in July or August, with exact dates dependant on wind conditions and published by **Tourism Bali** *(instagram.com/balitourismauthority)*.

Best Places for...

$ Budget $$ Midrange $$$ Top End

Eating

Talented Kitchens

Warung Mak Beng $

B1

No menu needed at this local favourite: the only option is its legendary *ikan laut goreng* (barbecued fish), which comes with sides and soup. Quick service. *9am-9pm*

Soul in a Bowl $$

A5

For good coffee and healthy breakfasts, fresh mains like rare tuna salad and plant-based sandwiches. *7am-11pm*

Massimo $$

8 B5

Like a breezy Milanese cafe inside, and a Balinese garden outside, this is *the* Sanur place for pizza. *11am-11pm*

Fisherman's Club $$$

C5

Classy seafood resto on Sanur's promenade, with comfy seating on the shady beach. Good kids' menu, too. *11.30am-11pm*

Tables with a View

Tities Warung $

10 B6

A good budget option on the beach, Tities serves up Indonesian classics, as well as sandwiches and snacks. Cash only. *8am-6pm*

Stuja di Pantai $$

11 B6

Chic all-day dining on Sanur's beachfront. Come for a morning coffee and Sanur's best pastries. Check out the nearby sea-turtle rescue tanks. *6am-10pm*

Soul on the Beach $$

C2

This breezy, laid-back cafe is a beachfront fave. It has an international menu with a focus on fresh, healthy meals. *7am-11pm*

Seagrass by the Beach $$

13 C5

Laid-back beachfront restaurant with pizzas, tacos, seafood platters and superb Indonesian curries. *7am-11pm*

Drinking

Drinks at the Beach

Byrd House Beach Club

C2

This elegant 'beach house' sprawls beneath towering palm trees; there's views of the beach and Gunung Agung. *6.30am-11pm*

Shotgun Social

B2

With 16 craft beers on tap, an extensive cocktail menu and a play area, this restaurant is great for families. *9am-11pm*

Costa by Monsta

B6

Mediterranean vibes on the beach, with white linen seats, fairy lights at night, and international wines and cocktails. *9am-10pm*

Casablanca

C3

No-frills restaurant in the eve, vibey dive club later – with live music (usually cover bands), sports and happy-hour specials. *5pm-1am*

See p113
for eating, drinking and shopping listings

Explore Denpasar & Around

Researched by Jade Bremner

Bali's sprawling and ever-growing capital of Denpasar has been the focus of much of the island's expansion and wealth over the past seven decades. Although its streets can be uncomfortably busy at times, there are tree-lined pockets to wander in the relatively affluent government and business district of Renon, where you'll discover a more genteel side.

Denpasar might not be the tropical paradise experience of other areas of Bali, but it's as much a part of life as the rice fields and beaches. This is the hub of the island for a million residents, and it has shopping malls, parks and vibrant markets, plus many cultural sights and good places to eat.

Getting Around

Car & Ridesharing

As Denpasar can be hot and dusty, it's unpleasant to walk or travel around by motorbike, so the most comfortable way to travel here is by car. Ridesharing apps make getting taxis easy. Major streets in Denpasar are often backed up with traffic during the day, so break up the misery with a stop at one of the city's many excellent restaurants.

Bus

On the off-chance you arrive in Bali by bus, Mengwi Bus Terminal is in the northwest corner of the city.

THE BEST

MUSEUM
Museum Negeri Propinsi Bali (p109)

FOOD MARKET
Pasar Badung (p112)

BALINESE HISTORY
Bajra Sandhi Monument (p112)

INDONESIAN EATS
Kedai Emak (p113)

SOCIAL IMPACT
Turtle Conservation and Education Centre (p112)

Pasar Bading (p112)
SUKHART/SHUTTERSTOCK

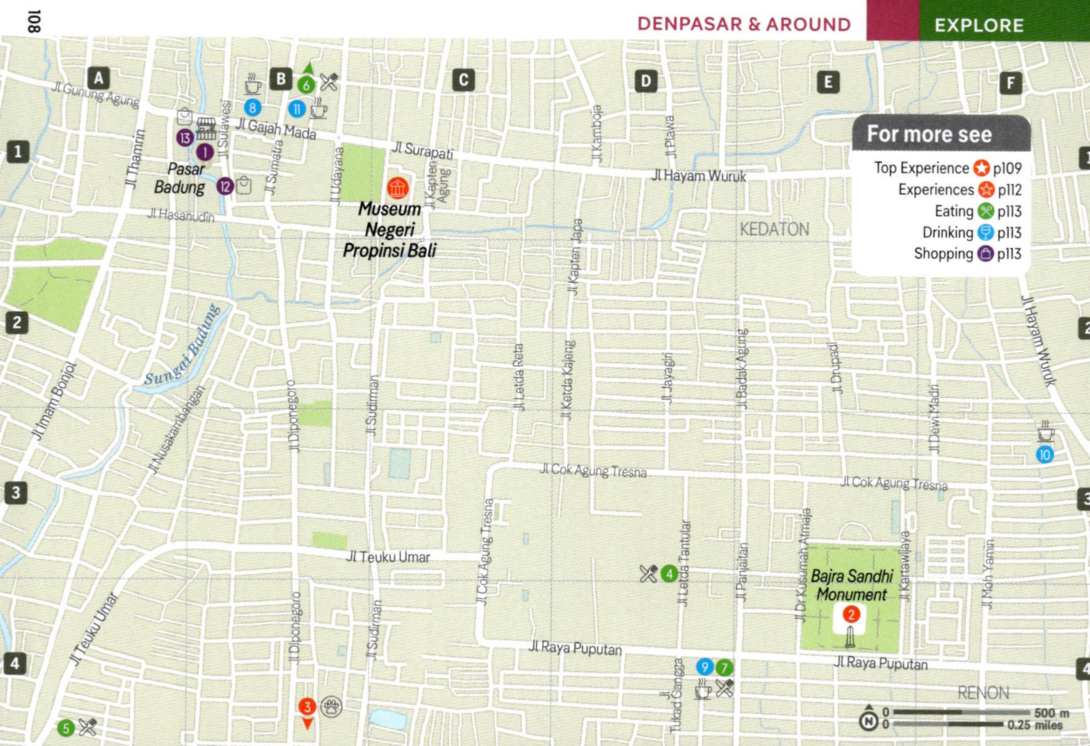
For more see
Top Experience p109
Experiences p112
Eating p113
Drinking p113
Shopping p113
Jl Gunung Agung
Jl Gajah Mada
Jl Sulawesi
Jl Sumatra
Jl Thamrin
Pasar Badung
Jl Hasanudin
Jl Udayana
Jl Surapati
Jl Kapten Agung
Museum Negeri Propinsi Bali
Jl Kamboja
Jl Plawa
Jl Hayam Wuruk
KEDATON
Jl Kapten Japa
Sungai Badung
Jl Imam Bonjol
Jl Nusakambangan
Jl Diponegoro
Jl Sudirman
Jl Letda Reta
Jl Ketda Kajeng
Jl Jayagiri
Jl Badak Agung
Jl Drupadi
Jl Dewi Madri
Jl Cok Agung Tresna
Jl Teuku Umar
Jl Letda Tantular
Jl Panjaitan
Jl Dr Kusumah Atmaja
Bajra Sandhi Monument
Jl Kartawijaya
Jl Moh Yamin
Jl Raya Puputan
Jl Tukad Gangga
RENON
0 500 m
0 0.25 miles

★ TOP EXPERIENCE

Museum Negeri Propinsi Bali

A record of Bali's unique culture and traditions is on display at Bali's oldest and largest museum, Museum Negeri Propinsi Bali *(adult/child 100,000/50,000Rp)*. Wander the four striking pavilions and explore a fascinating collection of relics and art.

MAP P108 **C1**

Ancient Discoveries

The museum is fascinating. Start chronologically in the **Gedung Timor** (East Building), which houses Stone Age tools and artefacts from different periods of Bali's history. Though the information shared here lacks context, it's a compelling collection.

Culture & Faith

Displays and explanations in the museum's three other buildings are more comprehensive: the **Buleleng Pavilion** focuses on coins and their use in rituals, as well as beautiful crafts and textiles. Displays at the **Karangasem Pavilion** focus on Balinese Hinduism, while the **Tabanan Pavilion** houses an impressive collection of kris, the ceremonial daggers that carry symbolic and spiritual value. It also houses dance costumes and masks, including a sinister *rangda* (an evil black-magic spirit of Balinese tales and dances), a healthy-looking Barong (a mythical lion-dog creature) and a towering Barong Landung (a really big Barong).

Architecture with Meaning

The courtyards, gates and pavilions showcase architectural styles from around Bali: the Tabanan Pavilion is constructed with posts from the court of a nobleman from Tabanan; the Karangasem Pavilion was built in the style of an audience hall from an East Bali palace; and the Buleleng Pavilion in the style of a North Bali residence.

PLANNING TIP
Skip the unofficial guides at the museum entrance; they add little value to a visit, and you're better off just reading the information panels, which include English-language content.

Walk Denpasar

Along the tree-lined streets of Denpasar's heart are windows into Balinese history and culture in the island's governmental and commercial centre. This short stroll takes in Denpasar's main museum, its largest traditional market and myriad other highlights.

START	END	LENGTH
Pasar Badung	Museum Negeri Propinsi Bali	1.25km; 3hr

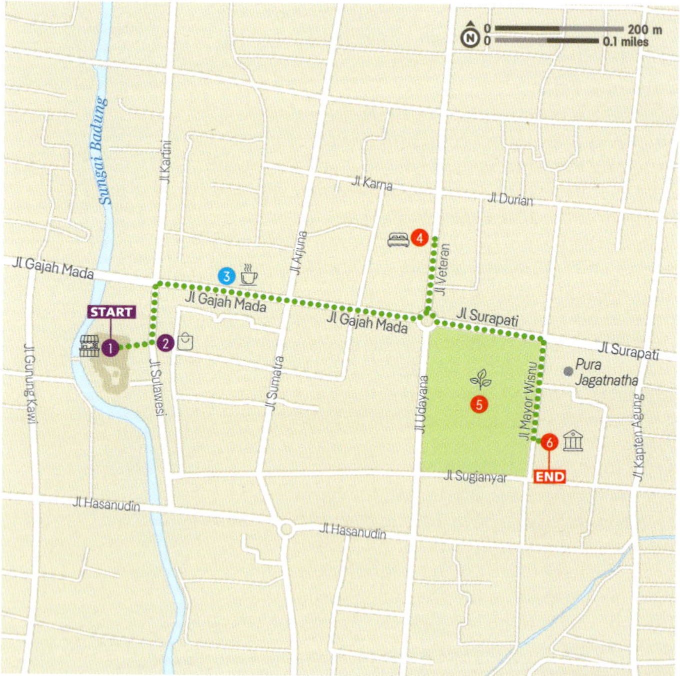

1 Start at the Market

The lively **Pasar Badung** (p112) is the largest market on the island. Get lost inside while browsing the floors of spices, fruit, vegetables, meat and homewares.

2 A Riot of Colour

Immediately east of Pasar Badung, Jl Sulawesi is home to a strip of fabric stores. The textiles here – batik, cottons, silks – come in colours that make Barbie look like an old purse. A good place to start is **Madju Batik Bali**. FYI: many shops are closed on Sunday.

3 Denpasar's Oldest Block

The block of Jl Gajah Mada, east of Jl Sulawesi, is as old as commercial Denpasar gets. Stop for a coffee at two-table **Bhineka Djaja** (p113), which has been roasting Bali-grown beans since 1935. Browse the shops catering to daily needs such as medicine, herbs, uniforms and sewing machines; if you have time, peep in at the wooden counters at **Toko Poon**.

4 Bali's Historic Hotel

The **Inna Bali Heritage Hotel** has a huge banyan tree, deep traditional verandas and a certain nostalgic charm. It dates from 1927 and was once the main tourist hotel on the island. Get the veteran employees talking – they have many stories. In the hotel's heyday (many, many decades ago), it hosted Charlie Chaplin, Queen Elizabeth II, Mahatma Gandhi and other luminaries.

5 Commemorative Square

Old Denpasar is centred on the park-like expanse of **Puputan Sq**. A statue of a family showing fortitude in the face of death recalls the suicidal stand of Bali's rajas against Dutch colonisers in 1906 (the word *puputan* means 'mass ritual suicide'). Just east, the elaborate **Pura Jagatnatha** is a recently renovated temple dedicated to the supreme god Sanghyang Widhi. It's a good example of the spatial arrangement that dictates the layout of all the temples on the island.

6 The Island's Museum

Finish at the **Museum Negeri Propinsi Bali** (p109), which holds among its treasures relics of the island's Stone Age past.

For an extraordinary guided tour of old Denpasar, book a walk with **I Gusti Ngurah Parta Wijaja** *(WhatsApp: +62 813 5322 0414)*, a lifelong Denpasar resident who explains the intricacies of Bali's culture, religion and history.

EXPERIENCES

Shop at Bali's Largest Market — TRADITIONAL MARKET

MAP: 1 P108 B1

The largest traditional trading place on the island, the imposing **Pasar Badung** feels distinctly different on each of its levels. There are spices on the ground floor; fruits, vegetables and meat on the 1st floor; and homewares and religious items on the 2nd floor. To see the colourful produce section in full swing, aim to be at the market between 8am and 10am. By 4pm, trading inside winds down and the action moves to the streets outside. In the southwest corner, scores of trucks laden with fresh produce jostle for space, and you'll find leafy greens and heaped baskets of tomatoes and onions, piles of dragon fruit, sweet potatoes and oranges. It's astounding watching the *tukang suun* – the women who transport the produce on behalf of buyers – carry heaped baskets weighing as much as 50kg on their heads.

Honour Bali's Independence — MONUMENT

MAP: 2 P108 E4

The imposing **Bajra Sandhi Monument** celebrates the resilience of the Balinese people and their struggle for independence from Dutch colonisers. The ornate structure, laden with symbolism, rises from the centre of a popular manicured park. Look for the 17 steps leading to the main entrance, count the eight pillars inside the monument, and notice that it stands at 45m tall. Together, these elements represent 17 August 1945 – Indonesia's Independence Day.

Adopt & Release Turtles — WILDLIFE SANCTUARY

MAP: 3 P108 B4

The well-run **Turtle Conservation and Education Centre** *(tcecserangan.jimdofree.com; by donation)* on Pulau Serangan is very active in rescuing and rehabilitating turtles. It offers visitors a chance to get up close to various species, but also to play a hands-on part in preserving one of Indonesia's most iconic marine species. Here, you'll see heart-wrenching sights like green turtles that have lost flippers to sharks or boat propellers, hawksbills recovering from operations to remove ingested plastic bags, and olive ridley turtles that were trapped in nets. You'll also see newly hatched youngsters jostling in some of the centre's many pools. The facility is free to visit, but you can pay 230,000Rp to 'adopt' a hatchling (during hatching season between April and September). You'll be given a coconut shell to transport your turtle, then taken by boat to the edge of the bay to release it.

LISTINGS

Best Places for...

$ Budget $$ Midrange $$$ Top End

See p108 for map of locations

Eating

Indonesian & Balinese

Kedai Emak $
4 D3
Contemporary Javanese restaurant serving buffet-style halal food. Fish, chicken and vegetarian options with fiery sauces. *8am-4pm*

Mie Goreng Makassar Pelita $
5 A4
Popular local eatery with a small menu of Sulawesi dishes. Come for the sublime sambal and generous portions. *11am-10pm*

Warung Wardani $

6
This Indonesian restaurant on Jl Yudistira is known for its delicious *nasi campur* (rice with a choice of side dishes) and chicken satay. *8am-5pm*

Babi Guling Renon $
7 D4
A slightly upscale *babi guling* (spit-roast pig) spot with excellent plate lunches of same. *9am-5pm*

Drinking

Coffee & Snacks

Bhineka Djaja

8 B1
This historic cafe has been serving traditional Balinese coffee since 1935. Come in for a cup and to buy a bag of Balinese coffee. *9am-3pm*

Bali Buda Renon

9 D4
Perfect for the health-conscious, this outlet of the Bali chain has a wide selection of smoothies and juices, as well as various milk options for coffee. *7am-9pm*

Gula Bali the Joglo

10 F3
A colourful, characterful cafe with a lovely garden. Lots of juices, teas and coffees. A good place to regroup after some hard-charging tourism. *10am-5pm*

Fuku

11 B1
A cosy, contemporary cafe known for its excellent specialty coffees and teas. Try the sea-salt latte. *8am-11pm*

Shopping

Timeless Buying

Jalan Sulawesi
12 B1
Translating to fabric street, and running beside Badung Market, this vibrant stretch is the place to get all kinds of textiles. *hours vary*

Kumbasari Art Market
13 A1
For artistic finds, wood carvings, baskets and Balinese handicrafts, head to this sprawling market on the Badung River. *24hr*

See p128
for eating,
drinking and
shopping
listings

Explore Ubud & Around

Researched by Marco Ferrarese

Ubud is where a short holiday can easily turn into a stay of weeks or even months. The town's reputation for art and culture is well deserved: this is a place imbued with Balinese traditions, where colourful offerings adorn the streets and the strains of gamelan are an ever-present soundtrack. But it's also somewhere relentlessly on trend – a showcase of sustainable design, mindfulness, culinary inventiveness and personal development, whether that's through yoga or a more esoteric pursuit.

Ubud is also suffocatingly popular, but there's always an escape into a gallery, a rice-field path, a hidden cafe. And the upside is that it draws creative people from around the world.

Getting Around

From South Bali, Ubud can be reached via Denpasar or Sanur. Expect the trip from the airport to take anywhere between 90 minutes to over two hours, depending on traffic.

Walking

The heart of Ubud is easily walkable – a top local activity.

Rideshares

The ubiquitous Gojek and Grab apps are how most visitors reach Ubud from the airport, and the easiest way to travel further afield.

Scooter/car rental

Renting a scooter or a car is inexpensive and practical, provided you can navigate heavy traffic and hilly roads.

THE BEST

EVENING ACTIVITY
Balinese dance performances (p118)

DAYTIME ACTIVITY
Ubud Monkey Forest (p120)

MUSEUM
Museum Puri Lukisan (p124)

GUIDED TOUR
Ubud Story Walks (p126)

HIDDEN TREASURE
Pura Penataran Sasih (p127)

Pura Taman Saraswati (p124)
SERGII FIGURNYI/SHUTTERSTOCK

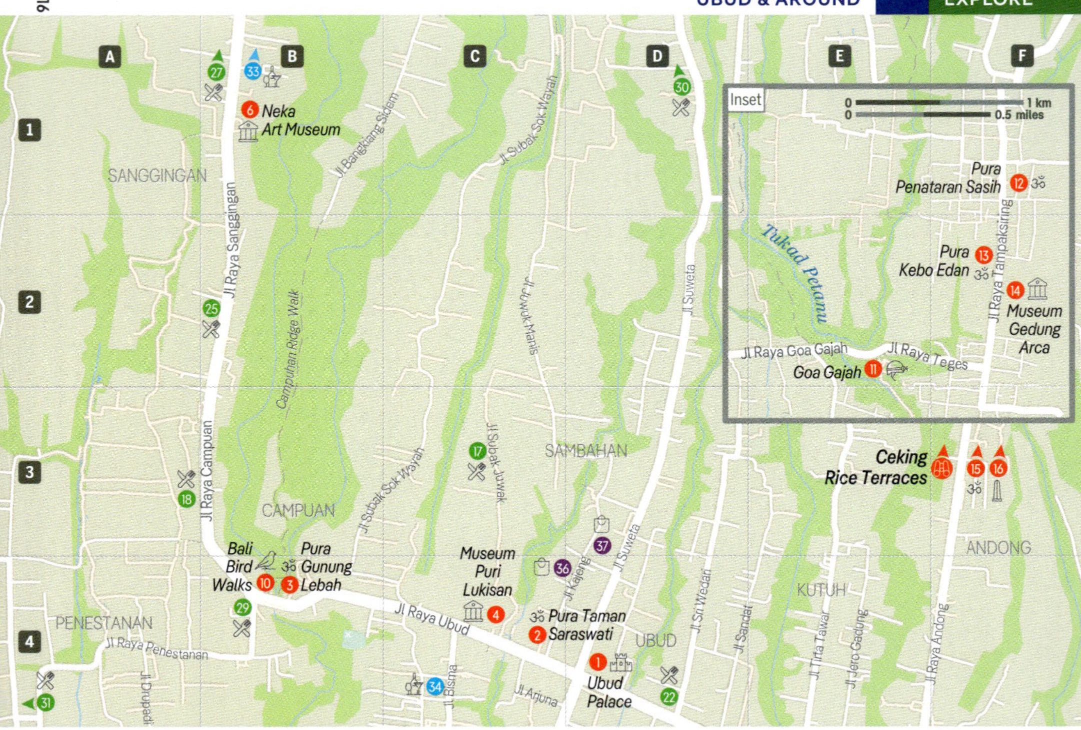
A
B
C
D
E
F
1
2
3
4
27
33
30
6 Neka Art Museum
SANGGINGAN
Jl Raya Sanggingan
Jl Bangkiang Sidem
Jl Subak Sok Wayah
Campuhan Ridge Walk
Jl Juwuk Manis
Jl Suweta
25
Inset
0 1 km
0 0.5 miles
Pura Penataran Sasih 12
Tukad Petanu
Pura Kebo Edan 13
14 Museum Gedung Arca
Jl Raya Tampaksiring
Jl Raya Goa Gajah
Jl Raya Teges
Goa Gajah 11
17
Jl Subak Juwak
SAMBAHAN
18
Jl Raya Campuan
CAMPUAN
Jl Subak Sok Wayah
Ceking Rice Terraces
15
16
37
ANDONG
Bali Bird Walks 10
Pura Gunung Lebah 3
Museum Puri Lukisan 4
36
Jl Kajeng
Jl Suweta
29
PENESTANAN
Jl Raya Penestanan
Jl Raya Ubud
Pura Taman Saraswati 2
UBUD
KUTUH
Jl Sri Wedari
Jl Sandat
Jl Tirta Tawar
Jl Jero Gadung
Jl Raya Andong
1 Ubud Palace
22
31
Jl Drupadi
34
Jl Bisma
Jl Arjuna

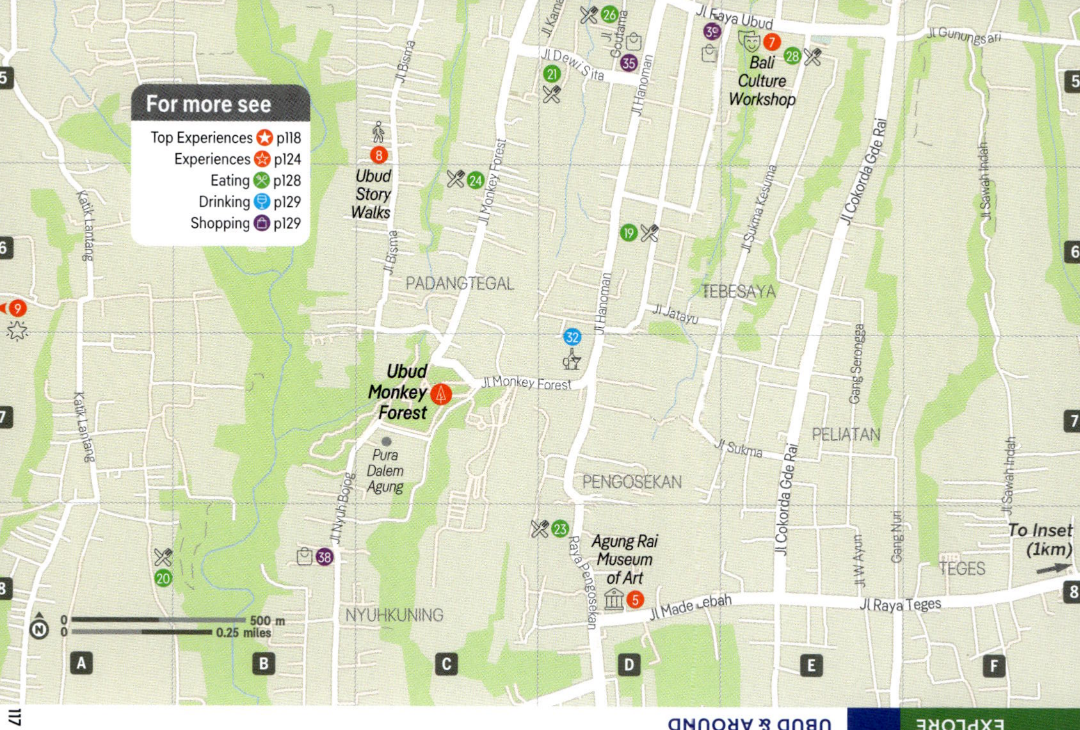
For more see
Top Experiences p118
Experiences p124
Eating p128
Drinking p129
Shopping p129
Ubud Story Walks
Bali Culture Workshop
PADANGTEGAL
TEBESAYA
Ubud Monkey Forest
Pura Dalem Agung
PENGOSEKAN
PELIATAN
Agung Rai Museum of Art
NYUHKUNING
TEGES
To Inset (1km)
Jl Raya Ubud
Jl Gunungsari
Jl Kama
Jl Goutama
Jl Dewi Sita
Jl Hanoman
Jl Bisma
Jl Monkey Forest
Jl Sukma Kesuma
Jl Cokorda Gde Rai
Jl Sawah Indah
Jl Jatayu
Gang Seronegga
Jl Sukma
Jl Nyuh Bojog
Raya Pengosekan
Jl Made Lebah
Jl Raya Teges
Jl W Ayun
Gang Nuri
Katik Lantang
500 m
0.25 miles
A
B
C
D
E
F
5
6
7
8

★ TOP EXPERIENCE

Balinese Dance Performances

Balinese dancers move with hypnotic grace as their dance tells stories rich with the essence of Hindu lore. A popular spot is Ubud Palace (Puri Saren Agung; p124), with Pura Taman Saraswati (p124) for Legong dance performances. The Agung Rai Museum of Art (p124) also hosts kecak performances on certain days. Gamelan music, played on bamboo and bronze instruments, is an integral part of many of the shows.

PLANNING TIP
Most of these nightly performances begin around 7pm and last about 90 minutes, but finding a schedule is challenging. Watch for signs at venues and buy tickets at the entrance.

Kecak Dance

Probably the best-known Balinese dance, the spellbinding kecak features a 'choir' of up to 80 men and boys who sit in concentric circles and slip into a trance as they chant and sing '*chak-a-chak-a-chak*', imitating a troop of monkeys. It's the only music to accompany the dance re-enactment from the Hindu epic, the Ramayana, which tells the ancient story of Prince Rama, Princess Sita, and the evil demon king, Rawana.

The modern version of kecak was developed in the 1930s through a collaboration between the Balinese dancer Wayan Limbak and the German painter Walter Spies.

Barong & Rangda

This dance enacts a battle between the good Barong, a dog-lion creature with huge eyes; and the evil Rangda (pictured), the monstrous Queen of Black Magic, with flames shooting out her ears and a mane of wild hair.

During the duel, the Barong's supporters draw their kris (traditional daggers) and rush in to help. The long-tongued, sharp-fanged Rangda throws

MUHAMAD MIFTAHUL/SHUTTERSTOCK

them into a trance, making them stab themselves. It's quite a spectacle. Thankfully, the Barong casts a spell that neutralises the kris, saving them from harm.

Because this sacred character is the benevolent protector of a village (you'll often see him in processions and rituals), the actors playing the Barong will emote a variety of winsome antics. But as is typical of Balinese dance, it is not all light-hearted.

Legong Dance

This most graceful and symbolic of Balinese dances is performed by two young girls dancing in mirror image. They are elaborately made up and dressed in gold brocade, relating a story about a king who takes a maiden captive and consequently starts a war, in which he dies.

QUICK BREAK
Snacks, water and beer are often sold inside the venues. Ladies with buckets of ice wait discreetly in the shadows. Ask for a cold one.

★ TOP EXPERIENCE

Ubud Monkey Forest

Ubud Monkey Forest was once a shady expanse home to three temples and a troop of over 1000 well-fed, light-fingered monkeys. Today, it's a top day-trip destination, with a flashy theme-park-like entrance and no semblance of a sacred place.

MAP P116 **C7**

PLANNING TIP
You can escape the worst of the crowds by visiting early or late in the day. Remember that the monkeys can smell any food: surrender it in case of an 'attack'.

Scan this QR code to book ahead.

Stick to the Essentials

Ignore stunts like the 'mysterious' tunnel at the entrance and follow the paths to the holiest of the temples, **Pura Dalem Agung**, where the entrance to the inner temple features Rangda figures devouring children.

Trails lead down a ravine to a cool and serene river valley. Although heavily promoted at the entrance, the attraction's app offers little to enhance a visit. Expect to spend about an hour visiting.

Beware of the Monkeys

You can't miss the grey-haired and greedy long-tailed Balinese macaques, who are nothing like the innocent-looking, doe-eyed primates in social-media images. They can bite, so be careful – the best course of action if they do is a full rabies treatment. Watch all your belongings carefully, including glasses, phones, bags and anything sticking out of your pockets. Never feed them, lest you set off a frenzy. If a monkey climbs on your bag or back, don't panic; if you don't carry food, it'll leave soon enough.

★ TOP EXPERIENCE

Ceking Rice Terraces

Heading north from Ubud, the stupendous views of the Ceking Rice Terraces from Tagallalang's main road are one of Bali's most scenic rice-terrace panoramas – but also the most visited. Find the beauty amid the barrage of cafes.

Make the Best of Your Visit

Visiting a place like the coffee plantation **Alas Harum** *(alasharum.com; entry only/pool access 50,000/200,000Rp)* is a good way to enjoy a sizeable chunk of Tegallalang's dramatic rice fields without many crowds, especially if you have kids in tow. For sure, the complex is posh and geared towards the many package tourists who come to lounge and swim in their large, cliff-hanging panoramic pools (only available to adult guests). There's also a restaurant, the ubiquitous swings and a zip line, each with additional fees.

Elsewhere, you'll be charged 25,000Rp to get down into the lush valley following any of the trails – plus the occasional toll levied by farmers.

Coping with Overtourism

Lower your expectations: the Ceking Rice Terraces are beautiful, but they are seriously overcrowded. Cafes competing for the best Instagram viewpoint continually expand over the edge of the cliff to cut off their competitors' views, which means most are obscured. Some have even added infinity pools. Signs and unofficial guides shill for parking lots, walking tours and the inevitable joints selling *kopi luwak* (civet coffee); avoid these due to animal cruelty.

MAP P116 **F3**

PLANNING TIP
Look for openings in the commercial strip not yet filled by cafes to savour the views of sinuous green ribbons without the hustle.

Scan this QR code for more information on Alas Harum.

WALKING TOUR

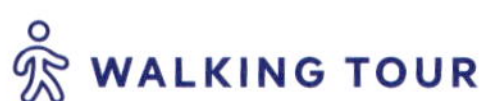

Walk Ubud

Starting in the heart of Ubud, this walk takes you into the sublime natural beauty of the surrounding area. Explore deep forests, lush rice fields and gushing waterfalls, all just north of town but feeling a world away. The route is fairly flat, but wear sturdy footwear for the more slippery areas.

START	END	LENGTH
Jl Kajeng	Jl Raya Ubud	7.5km; 3hr

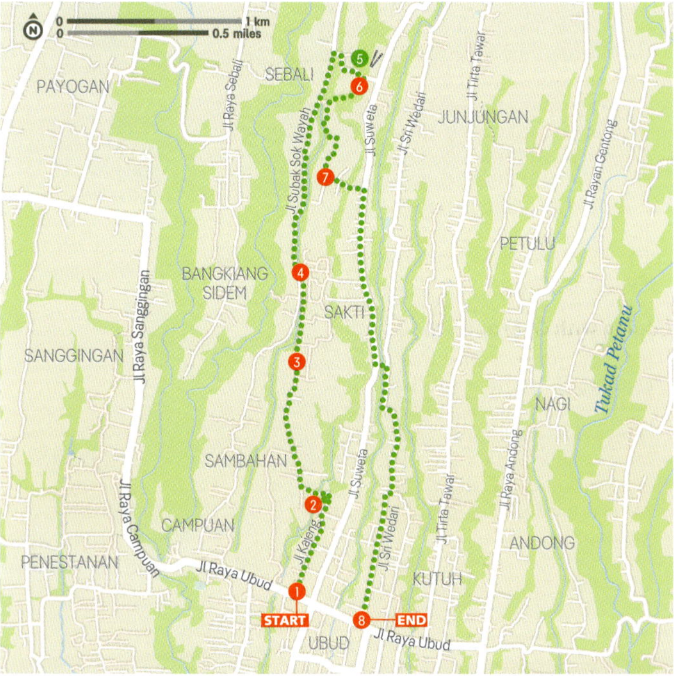

1 Festival of Vendors

Head north up **Jl Kajeng**, passing by the long strips of vendor stalls. Amid the tat, look for handmade items demonstrating the sellers' artistry. Note the hundreds of concrete paving squares, each decorated by a local sponsor. Many are quite sweet.

2 Drink a Coconut

Just past the **Bale Banjar Ubud Kaja**, head uphill as the road becomes a path. You'll soon see a lush green vista of rice fields. Follow the path north past a few villas and vendors selling coconuts. Stop off for a fresh one to rehydrate. The cement path will soon give way to dirt.

3 Rice Irrigation

Eventually, the path will morph into the top of a narrow concrete wall that runs along a **subak (irrigation) channel** on one side and a small river on the other. Palm trees and bamboo close in overhead, providing deep shade.

4 Fields of Green

Walk carefully until you come to a **tiny footbridge**. Cross over it and follow the path up the embankment. Continue north for about 1.5km, through green ricefields dotted with the odd villa, vendor and artist's studio. Look for relaxed, family-run guesthouses where you could easily lose a few weeks.

5 Cafe & Waterfalls

When you reach a road wide enough for cars, turn east. Walk down, past **Cafe Bintang** (if open, enjoy a casual Japanese meal here), to a bridge over surging **waterfalls**, which flow year-round.

6 Lush River Gorge

To the east of Cafe Bintang, take the small lane that runs south through the **river gorge**. Fenced yards filled with ducks give way to more rice fields as the path rises up out of the gorge and curves south.

7 Small Lanes & Cafes

After about 750m of walking through the small gorge, turn east and follow the car-capable road down, over a bridge and back up to Jl Suweta. Walk south for 1km, past many small cafes – perfect for a pause.

8 Meandering Downhill

Cross the bridge from Jl Suweta to fairly quiet Jl Sri Wedari and walk gently downhill past little warungs (food stalls), cafes and shops, back to Jl Raya Ubud.

EXPERIENCES

Visit Ubud Palace PALACE

MAP: 1 P116 **D4**

The modest **Ubud Palace** *(free)* and its temple, **Puri Saren Agung**, share a compound in the heart of Ubud. Most of the structures were built after the 1917 earthquake, and the local royal family still lives here. Despite the name, this sprawling compound is not palatial or excessively ornate. Rather, it's a warren of courtyards and traditional Balinese buildings that extend well back from the limited area that's open to the public. It's a popular venue for Balinese dance performances (p118).

Experience Ubud's Evocative Temples HINDU TEMPLES

While most of Ubud's dozens of temples are closed to visitors, there are some noteworthy exceptions. **Pura Taman Saraswati** (MAP: 2 P116 **C4**; *ubudwaterpalace.com; adult/child 35,000/25,000Rp*), one of the most picturesque, is always open to the public. Right off Jl Raya Ubud, it's a welcome relief from the crowded footpaths. Water flowing from the rear of the site feeds a pond in front, which overflows with lotus blossoms.

Just west of the centre, by the start of Jl Raya Campuan, **Pura Gunung Lebah** (MAP: 3 P116 **B4**; *free*) sits on a jutting rock at the confluence of two tributaries of Sungai Cerik. Far below street level in a lush gorge, the setting is magical.

Explore Bali's Artistic Offerings ART MUSEUM

MAP: 4 P116 **C4**

The modern Balinese art movement began in Ubud when artists started to abandon traditional religious and royal themes for scenes of everyday life. A highlight of the local art museums, **Museum Puri Lukisan** *(purilukisanmuseum.com; adult/child 95,000Rp/free)*, displays works from all schools and periods of Balinese art. You can easily spend an hour or two here.

The **East Building** has a collection of early works from Ubud and the surrounding villages. The **North Building** features fine ink drawings by I Gusti Nyoman Lempad (1862–1978) and paintings by artists of the Pita Maha School, such as Walter Spies (1895–1942). Don't miss *Temple Festival* (1938) by I Gusti Ketut Kobot (1917–99).

Discover Masterpieces ART MUSEUM

MAP: 5 P116 **D8**

The **Agung Rai Museum of Art** *(ARMA; armabali.com/museum; adult/student/child under 7 150,000Rp/75,000Rp/free)* is another must-see museum. Founder Agung Rai built his fortune by selling Balinese art to foreigners in the 1970s. As a dealer, he acquired one of Indonesia's most impressive private art collections. Exhibits include classical Kamasan paintings and Batuan-style works from the 1930s and '40s. In the traditional gallery, look for *The Dance Drama Arja* (1990) by I Ketut Kasta (b 1945), *Cremation Ceremony* (1994) by I Ketut Sepi (b 1941) and the extraordinarily detailed *Wali 'Ekadesa Rudra'* (2015) by I Wayan Mardiana (b 1970).

Understand Ubud's Artistic Reputation

ART MUSEUM

MAP: 6 P116 **B1**

The **Neka Art Museum** *(nekaart museum.com; adult/student & child 150,000Rp/75,000Rp)* offers an excellent introduction to Balinese art, with a top-notch collection. On a one-hour visit, don't miss the multiroom **Balinese Painting Hall**, which showcases the *wayang* (puppet) style, as well as the European-influenced Ubud and Batuan styles, which evolved in the 1920s and '30s. Also notable is the **Lempad Pavilion**, with works by the master artist, sculptor and architect I Gusti Nyoman Lempad (1862–1978).

Experience Balinese Shadow Puppetry

PUPPET SHOWS

MAP: 7 P116 **E5**

More than entertainment, *wayang kulit* (shadow-puppet plays) have been Bali's candlelit village cinema for centuries, embodying all the sacred seriousness of a classical Greek drama. Traditional performances were typically long and intense, lasting six hours or more.

Originally used to bring ancestors back to this world, the shows feature painted buffalo-hide puppets believed to have great spiritual power, and the *dalang* (puppeteer and storyteller) is an almost mystical figure. In central Ubud, **Bali Culture Workshop** *(baliculture workshop.com; 100,000Rp)*, at Oka Kartini BnB, stages popular evening shows.

UBUD'S ARTISTIC HISTORY

Late in the 19th century, the Sukawati royal family established an outpost in Ubud and began a series of alliances and confrontations with neighbouring kingdoms. In 1900, along with the kingdom of Gianyar, Ubud became (at its own request) a Dutch protectorate and was able to concentrate on its religious and cultural life. The royals encouraged visits by Western artists in the 1930s, most notably Walter Spies, Colin McPhee and Rudolf Bonnet. They provided an enormous stimulus to local art by introducing new ideas and displaying and promoting Balinese culture worldwide. As mass tourism arrived in Bali, Ubud became an important art-and-culture destination.

UBUD'S BEST EVENTS

Bali Spirit Festival
A popular yoga, dance and music festival that typically takes place in early May, featuring hundreds of workshops, concerts, wellness activities and more. *balispirit festival.com*

Ubud Village Jazz Festival
For over a decade, this annual two-day jazz festival in late July has featured Indonesian groups and an international lineup of performers. *ubudvillagejazzfestival.com*

Ubud Writers & Readers Festival
Southeast Asia's major literary event draws many famous writers and readers from around the world for a five-day celebration in October. *ubudwritersfestival.com*

Walk & Cycle Ubud GUIDED TOURS

Specialised tours in Ubud include thematic walks and cultural adventures. Perhaps the best two to three hours you'll spend is on a tour with **Ubud Story Walks** (MAP: 8 P116 **C5**; *ubudsyorywalks.com; from 350,000Rp*). These remarkably detailed and entertaining tours cover Balinese culture and history in the region.

You can also whizz downhill while enjoying day-long tours of remote villages near Ubud with **Banyan Tree Bike Tours** (MAP: 9 P116 **A6**; *banyantreebike tours.com; adult/child from 920,000/585,000Rp*). The popular tours emphasise interaction with villagers.

One of Ubud's first tourist businesses, **Bali Bird Walks** (MAP: 10 P116 **B4**; *balibirdwalk.com; from 670,000Rp*) was started by the legendary Victor Mason more than 30 years ago. You're likely to spot between 30 and 100 species on a bird-watching tour.

Enter a Cave Temple at Goa Gajah HINDU TEMPLE

MAP: 11 P116 **E2**

Visitors enter the rock-hewn **Goa Gajah**, *(adult/child 50,000/25,000Rp)*, or 'Elephant Cave' just outside Ubud, through what resembles the cavernous mouth of a demon. Inside, there are fragmentary remains of a lingam (the phallic symbol of the Hindu god Shiva) and a yoni (the vaginal symbol of the Hindu goddess Shakti), as well as a statue of Shiva's son, the elephant-headed god, Ganesha. Outside, two square bathing pools feature waterspouts held by six female figures.

Venture to Pejeng's Remarkable Relic ANCIENT ARTIFACT

MAP: 12 P116 **F1**

Located 5km east of central Ubud, the village of Pejeng was the capital of the Balinese Pejeng kingdom for a short period between Javanese invasions. It collapsed in 1343 CE when the Majapahits – a Javanese Hindu dynasty – defeated King Dalem Bedaulu. Today, it is home to one of the region's most extraordinary but least-visited sights.

Pura Penataran Sasih *(by donation)* was once the state temple of the Pejeng kingdom. In the inner courtyard is a remarkable treasure: a huge bronze drum known as the **Moon of Pejeng**, which is believed to date back to as early as 300 BCE. The hourglass-shaped drum is 186cm high and is the largest single-piece cast drum in the world. The bronze alloy and casting technique have been traced back to the Dong Son people of ancient Vietnam, revealing a previously unknown trade route.

See the Giant of Pejeng

ANCIENT STATUE

Across the road from Pura Penataran Sasih, **Pura Kebo Edan** (MAP: 13 P116 **F2**) is not an imposing structure, but it *is* famous for its much-weathered, 3m-high statue, known as the **Giant of Pejeng**, thought to be approximately 600 years old. Details are sketchy, but it may represent Bima, a hero of the Mahabharata, dancing on a dead body, as in a myth related to the Hindu Shiva cult.

Many of the oldest Pejeng treasures have been found by farmers ploughing their fields. See a range of artefacts at the **Museum Gedung Arca** (MAP: 14 P116 **F2**). Ubud Story Walks also runs an excellent tour of Pejeng's main sites.

Visit Bali's Iconic Water Temple

HINDU TEMPLE

MAP: 15 P116 **F3**

Immediately east and in the shadow of the presidential palace, **Pura Tirta Empul** *(tirtaempultemple.com; adult/child 75,000Rp/50,000Rp)* dates to 962 CE. This water temple is believed to possess magical powers, and the holy springs bubble up into a large pool, gushing out through waterspouts into a *petirtaan* (bathing area).

Explore Gunung Kawi

ANCIENT MONUMENT

MAP: 16 P116 **F3**

One of Bali's oldest, holiest and most important monuments, the stunning river-valley complex of **Gunung Kawi** *(adult/child 75,000Rp/50,000Rp)*, 13km north of Ubud, consists of 10 huge *candi* (shrines) cut out of the rock face. Each is believed to be a memorial to a member of an 11th-century Balinese royal family. Legends relate that the mighty fingernails of revered warrior Kebo Iwa carved the whole group.

Get to Gunung Kawi as early as possible: start down the 250 steps by 7.30am to see residents going about their morning routines.

LISTINGS

Best Places for...

$ Budget $$ Midrange $$$ Top End

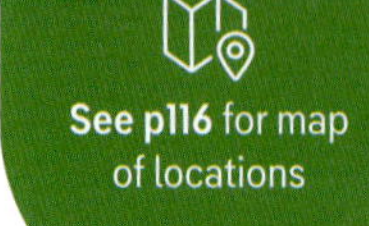

Eating

Classic Ubud Cafes

Sweet Orange Warung $

C3

An idyllic location in the midst of the rice fields; walk here via the path to the right of Museum Puri Lukisan (p124). *8am-9pm*

Yellow Flower Cafe $

18 A3

Perched in Penestanan along a greenery-edged path, with a range of health drinks and coffees. Incredible views. *7am-9pm*

Kafe $

D6

Attractive decor, new-agey vibe and healthy food are the hallmarks of this upscale cafe; alt-healer promotions cover the bulletin board. *7am-11pm*

Hidden Space Ubud Cafe $$

20 A8

Chilled cafe with good food, delicious cold-pressed juices, and a quiet area to pull out the laptop and work. *9am-6pm Mon-Sat*

Fancy Meals

Nusantara $$$

21 D5

From the legendary Locavore team, a stylish Indonesian restaurant with boldly flavoured, highly spiced dishes. *noon-2.30pm & 6-9.30pm Tue-Sun, 6-9.30pm Mon*

Hujan Locale $$$

22 D4

Chef Will Meyrick's Ubud outpost serves Indonesian food with creative flair in an open-air, vintage dining room. *noon-3pm & 5.30pm-10pm*

Merlin's $$$

D8

An immersive and exclusive (reservations necessary) mystical dining experience paired with magic, where the food 'chooses you' according to tarot cards you draw. *2-11pm*

Honey & Smoke $$$

24 C6

Everything here is flame-grilled with centuries-old Ottoman fire-and-smoke techniques. *noon-11pm*

Balinese Food

Warung Pulau Kelapa $$

25 B2

Huge menu of authentic Indonesian dishes from across the archipelago. Sensational sambal; ask for dishes 'local style' to get spicy. *10am-11pm*

Compound Warung $

26 D5

Behind a family guest-house on delightful Jl Goutama, serving bargain dishes bursting with flavour and style. Bunnies hop about the garden. *11am-10pm*

Nasi Ayam Kedewatan Ibu Mangku $

B1

Few residents trekking through Sayan pass without stopping. The star is *sate lilit* – minced, spiced meat pressed onto skewers. *7am-5pm*

Vegetarian & Vegan Meals

Sayuri Healing Food Cafe & Academy $$

28 E5

Restaurant, community and cooking academy promoting raw-vegan food culture with Japanese chef Sayuri Tanaka. *8am-11pm*

Zest $$

 B4

Peaceful bohemian cafe with a delightful forest view, serving global cuisine made with farm-to-table, fine ingredients. *8am-10pm*

Raw Temple $$

 D1

Vegan sanctuary serving detox juices and inventive raw dishes, and hosting weekly musical and transformative experiences. *9am-11am*

Moksa $$

 A4

On a permaculture farm, serves extraordinary meals created with simple vegetables. Many dishes are raw. Bucolic setting. *10am-9pm*

Drinking

Cocktail Bars

Ibu Susu Bar & Kitchen

 D7

Excellent, well-presented cocktails, such as the Pomelo Negroni, which fuse Southeast Asian flavours with international mixology. *noon-midnight*

Kawi

 B1

Inventive drinks made with local ingredients like *arak* (distilled palm wine). Narrow bar, chill garden. *7pm-midnight Sun-Fri*

Why Not

 C4

A feel-good, packed beer bar with daily live rock, blues and reggae bands, plus cocktails. *3pm-midnight*

Shopping

Made in Ubud

Ananda Soul

 D5

Locally designed and produced jewellery (and small line of resort-wear) whose proceeds support local communities. *10am-9pm*

Toko Elami

36 C4

Over 20 local artisans' creations are sold here amid the Jl Kajeng market. Look for extraordinary T-shirts, prints, bags and more. *9am-9pm*

Unique to Ubud

Threads of Life

37 D3

Famous purveyor of traditional textiles. The Jl Kajeng location is joined by a large shop on Jl Raya Lungsiakan. *10am-6pm*

Tradisi Textiles

 B8

South of Ubud Monkey Forest (p120), this workshop with retail space has artisans producing traditional ikat and other textiles. *9am-6pm*

Ganesha Bookshop

39 D5

Extraordinary curated selection of new and used titles, with a huge range on Balinese and Indonesian culture and works by authors appearing at the Ubud Writers & Readers Festival (p126). *9am-9pm*

See p139
for eating
and shopping
listings

Explore East Bali

Researched by Narina Exelby

Exploring East Bali is one of the island's great pleasures. Rice terraces spill down hillsides under swaying palms, wild volcanic beaches are washed by pounding surf and age-old villages soldier on with barely a trace of modernity. Watching over it all is Gunung Agung (3142m), the active volcano known to the Balinese as the place where the gods reside.

Temples, palaces and water gardens are dotted throughout the landscape. You'll find traces of Bali's past amid evocative ruins in the former royal city of Klungkung; explore its underwater delights around Amed; trek through patchwork paddies around Sidemen and, on the northeast coast, discover an enchanting region where tourism is barely known.

Getting Around

Car

East Bali is all about exploring, and you can never get too lost here – there's always another surprise around the corner, be it a waterfall, view, temple or village. While you can rely on one of Bali's ride-hailing apps (Grab, GoJek or BlueBird) to get you into East Bali, you'll need to have your own wheels to have the freedom to discover the region's untrod beaches, pristine waterfalls, remote sacred temples and timeless villages. If you have an idea of where you want to go, you can usually arrange a private driver through your accommodation.

THE BEST

ADVENTUROUS HIKE
Gunung Agung (p137)

DIVING
Pantai Amed (p137)

CULTURAL CONNECTION
Samsara Living Museum (p135)

DAY WALKS
Sidemen (p136)

TEMPLE
Pura Besakih (p136)

Rice fields with Gunung Agung (p137) in the background
NICK N A/SHUTTERSTOCK

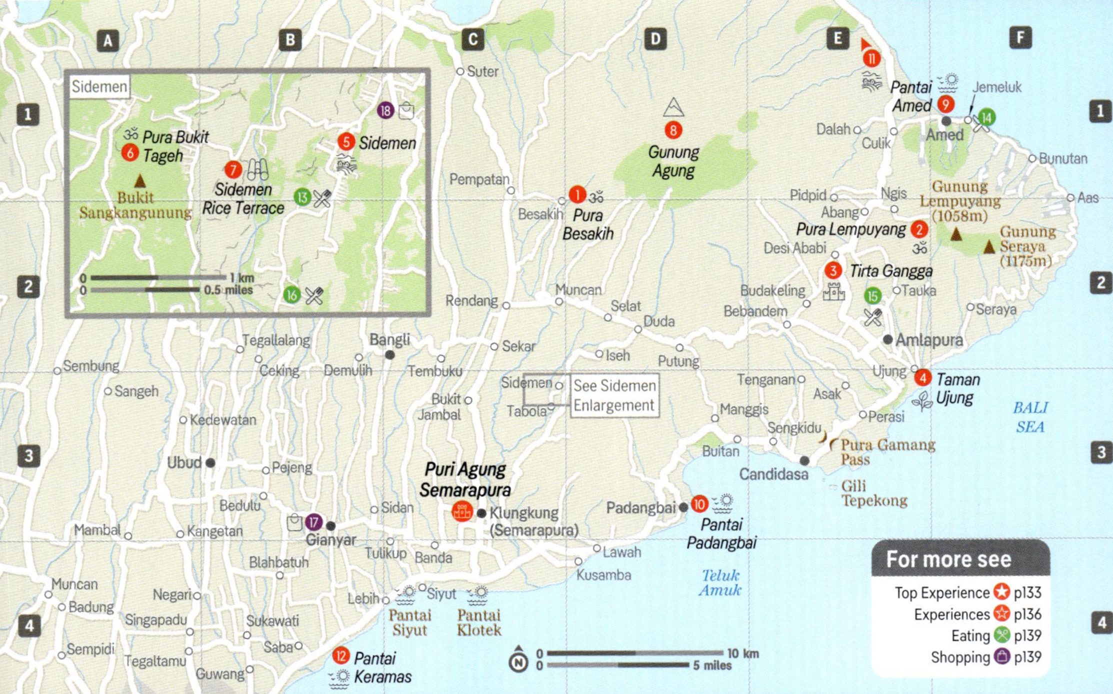

For more see
Top Experience p133
Experiences p136
Eating p139
Shopping p139

★ TOP EXPERIENCE

Puri Agung Semarapura

Klungkung (officially called Semarapura) is home to the historic Puri Agung Semarapura (Klungkung Palace). The palace compound remains as a reminder of the town's royal past as the centre of Bali's most important kingdom.

Legacies of the Rajas

Begin at the **Museum Semarajaya** on the western side of the compound. Among the highlights is an evocative painting depicting the Klungkung monarchy's 1908 *puputan* (ritual suicide; p135), courtesy of the Dutch troops. Displays include ceremonial items, traditional weapons and clothing.

Klungkung Palace

Now fully briefed on the Klungkung royals, you can delve into the fascinating remains of Puri Agung Semarapura. Built in 1710, the compound was laid out as a large square, with courtyards, gardens, pavilions and moats. Much was destroyed in 1908.

Evocative Art

Next up is the **Bale Kambang**, a beautiful, water-surrounded, open-sided pavilion. The ceiling showcases rows of paintings depicting the astrological calendar, folk tales and legends.

Supreme Court

In the northeastern corner of the complex, the airy **Kertha Gosa** pavilion was effectively the supreme court of the Klungkung kingdom. A superb example of Klungkung architecture, it features a ceiling covered with fine 20th-century paintings in *wayang* (shadow-puppet) style.

MAP P132 **C3**

PLANNING TIP

You'll need about an hour to explore this whole compound. Buy your entrance ticket over the road at the Puputan Monument (p135). The ticket covers entrance to the monument as well as the palace, so take a look around there first.

Drive East Bali

Take time to explore some of East Bali's most historic places, and you'll come away with a deeper understanding and appreciation of the events and traditions that have shaped this unique island. Give yourself a full day to explore this route, stopping for lunch at a cafe in seaside Candidasa.

START	END	LENGTH
Penglipuran	Samsara Living Musem	80km; 1 day

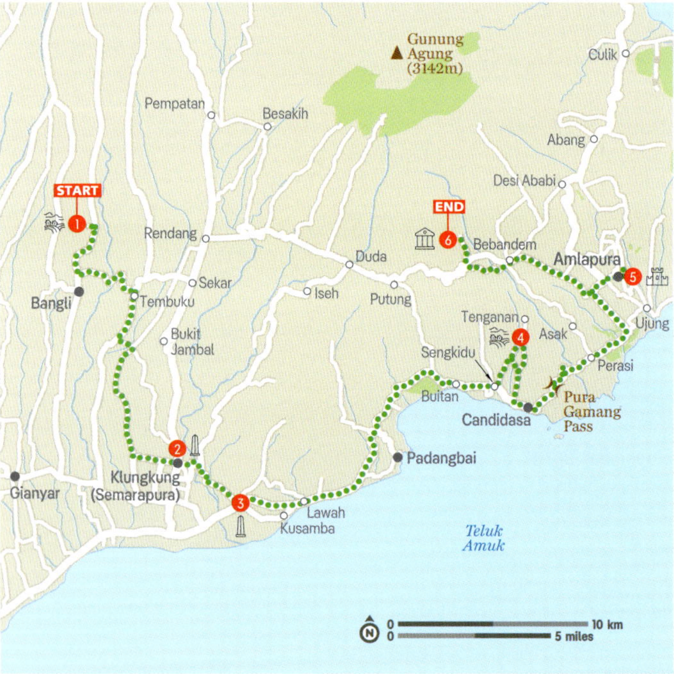

1 Wander a Traditional Village

Penglipuran *(penglipuran.com; adult/child 50,000/30,000Rp)* was established in the 14th century and retains a traditional village layout, with family compounds branching off a pedestrian avenue. Visitors can visit compounds with QR codes at the entrances for more information. Don't miss the 500m-long boardwalk through the nearby bamboo forest.

2 Monument to Royal Sacrifice

Klungkung was the last Balinese kingdom to succumb to the Dutch in 1908, and the sacrifice of its royal family, who died by *puputan* (ritual suicide) rather than surrender, is commemorated in the towering **Puputan Monument** *(adult/child 50,000Rp/25,000Rp)*. Reliefs here also depict other important historic events including battles with the Dutch.

3 Statue of a Balinese Heroine

Along the east coast, where Jl Rama (leading from Klungkung) intersects with the coastal highway, look out for the statue of **Ida I Dewa Agung Istri Kanya**. This Balinese heroine is celebrated for leading the Klungkung army to victory in the battle against the Dutch at Kusamba in 1849.

4 Explore Bali Aga villages

Tenganan Pegringsingan and **Tenganan Dauh Tukad** *(by donation)*, separated by a small valley, are village homes to descendants of the Bali Aga, the island's earliest inhabitants. A visit to either is a chance to learn about Bali Aga traditions and, while they're both car-free and laid out as they have been for centuries (with homes leading off a central walkway), the two villages offer quite different and rewarding visitor experiences.

5 Visit a Royal Palace

Puri Agung Karangasem *(instagram.com/puriagung karangasem; 30,000Rp)* is still home to the descendants of the royal family, but visitors are welcome to explore a lovingly kept part of it. Entry to the tranquil palace is past beautifully sculpted panels and an impressive multi-tiered gate; once inside you'll see architectural influences from Europe, China and Bali. A highlight of the manicured grounds is the Bale Kambang, an ornate floating pavilion surrounded by a large pond.

6 Experience Traditional Ways of Life

The outstanding, community-run **Samsara Living Museum** *(samsarabali.com; 100,000Rp)* in Jungutan offers an engaging, well-curated window into Balinese culture and daily life. Book via the website for a **cooking class** *(900,000Rp)*, **dance lesson** *(375,000Rp)* or other cultural experiences.

EXPERIENCES

Visit Bali's Holiest Temple

HINDU TEMPLE

MAP: 1 P132 **D1**

Bali's most important temple, **Pura Besakih** *(besakih.org; 150,000Rp)* stands on the southwestern slope of Gunung Agung, nearly 1000m above sea level. It is a vast collection of 23 separate but related temples that together form a landing complex for the gods on Bali.

Individual temples are not always open to visitors, but your guide (included in the ticket price) will show you around the complex. Some might try to keep your tour short – so insist on following the path to the back of Pura Besakih, as the view of scores of jet-black *meru* (multi-roofed shrines) soaring towards the sky is striking. For a fantastic view over Bali head up to Pura Gelap.

See Bali's iconic Gates of Heaven

HINDU TEMPLE

MAP: 2 P132 **E2**

Pura Lempuyang is where you can get *that* iconic Bali photo: the one with mighty Gunung Agung framed by *candi bentar* (split gates), you posing between them, and the whole scene is reflected in in a mirror.

It's actually a complex of seven temples, and the largest and most easily accessed is Pura Penataran Lempuyang, where you'll queue for hours to be photographed. The temple is open from 5am; it costs 50,000Rp for the compulsory shuttle there, and entry is 70,000Rp.

Wander the Water Gardens

HISTORIC PLACES

Wander between pretty koi ponds dotted with statues at **Tirta Gangga** (MAP: 3 P132 **E2**; *tirtaganggabali.com; 90,000Rp*), a picturesque water garden north of Puri Agung Karangasem (p135). Built in 1946 for the last raja of Karangasem, there are fountains and flowers, bridges, stepping stones and even a small pool that you can bathe in. Tirta Gangga gets incredibly busy, so aim to get here early (gates open at 6am).

Taman Ujung (MAP: 4 P132 **E3**; *instagram.com/tamansoekasada ujung; 100,000Rp*), another water palace, is a 20-minute drive south from Tirta Gangga. It is far more simple in design, but its geometry makes it incredibly striking – particularly when the water in the three large ponds is still, and reflects the surrounding bridges and pavilions.

Trek Around Rural Sidemen

TREKKING

Sidemen (MAP: 5 P132 **B1**) charms visitors with its rural setting, and most hosts can arrange a local guide to lead you on walking trails through the valley. For something more challenging, ask your guide to take you to **Pura Bukit Tageh** (MAP: 6 P132 **A1**), the shrine at the top of the hill that rises on the west side of Sidemen. It's a four-hour circular hike with gorgeous views of Gunung Agung and, on clear days, the ocean too.

Stroll Sidemen's Rice Terrace

VILLAGE HIKE

MAP: 7 P132 **B1**

On the western fringe of Sidemen, visitors can walk a trail around the village **rice terrace** *(instagram .com/sidemenriceterrace; 25,000Rp)*. This circular 3km trail, managed by a community organisation, is well signposted and can easily be walked on your own. **Guides** *(1hr 100,000Rp)* are available if you want someone to share more details on the area.

Summit Bali's Highest Mountain

TREKKING

MAP: 8 P132 **D1**

Scaling **Gunung Agung** (3142m), Bali's highest and most sacred mountain, is one of the island's most physically challenging adventures – but watching sunrise from up here is an extremely profound experience.

The two most popular routes start from **Pura Pasar Agung Sebudi** (on Agung's southern slope) and **Pura Besakih** (on the southwest). It'll take four or five hours to summit Agung via the shorter, more direct route from Pura Pasar Agung Sebudi, while the tougher route from Pura Besakih takes six or seven.

Most accommodation in the region can recommend hiking guides (you cannot climb Agung without one); two very experienced guides are **Wayan Tegteg** *(WhatsApp +62 813 3852 5677)* and **I Ketut Uriada** *(WhatsApp +62 812 364 6426)*.

Dive & Snorkel the East Coast

DIVING

Bali's eastern coastline is revered for its exquisite underwater delights. Around laid-back **Pantai Amed** (MAP: 9 P132 **F1**), snorkelling highlights include the coral gardens of Jemeluk Bay and Pantai Selang. The area is a freediving hub and home to numerous dive companies, and the dive sites off Jemeluk, Lipah and Selang beaches feature slopes and drop-offs with soft and hard corals and abundant fish. The well-known *Liberty* wreck site at Tulamben is a 20-minute drive from Amed.

Further south there's good diving around **Pantai Padangbai** (MAP: 10 P132 **D3**). The most popular spots are Blue Lagoon and Teluk Jepun, which have a range of soft and hard corals and marine life including sharks, turtles and wrasse. Many of Padangbai's dive centres (find them on Jl Silayukti, past the fast-ferry pier) also offer trips to nearby **Gili Tepekong** and **Gili Biaha**, as well as to **Tulamben** and **Nusa Penida**.

DECODING AMED

Although Amed is one small village, its name nowadays covers the neighbouring bays and fishing villages of Jemeluk (which has a buzzing travellers strip), Banutan (with both a beach and headlands) and Lipah (which has a lively mix of cafes). Tourism development – and the name Amed – have also extended through Lehan, Selang, Banyuning, Aas and on to Kusambi. For accommodation, you'll need to choose between the villages (puts you right on the sand) and the sunny headlands (for sweeping ocean vistas).

Chill out in Tejakula VILLAGES

As you travel the coastline towards Lovina, the lovely villages of **Tejakula and Les** (MAP: 11 P132 **E1**) are well worth an overnight stop, at least. Around here, tucked between the banana and palm trees that fringe the lanes to the beach and the hills, you'll find enticing boutique resorts, retreats and creative cafes that are hidden away like well-kept secrets. Add the chance to book a cooking class at **Dapur Bali Mula** *(instagram.com/dapurbalimula; 450,000Rp)*, to dive and snorkel without crowds, and to watch fishing boats launching at sunset, and you've reasons to linger here for days.

Surf at Pantai Keramas SURFING

MAP: 12 P132 **B4**

Set along a slowly developing stretch of Bali's lower eastern coastline is **Pantai Keramas**, a black-sand beach with a powerful, consistent break that's revered among surfers. The fast-barrelling right-hand reef break, which was a location on the World Surf League Championship Tour in 2019, is watched over by **Komune Beach Club** *(komuneresorts.com)*. The resort erected permanent, powerful floodlights that illuminate the break at night and before dawn – it's an exceptional experience limited to six people at a time (you must book in advance through Komune Resort), and a thrill to watch from the beach club.

Not far from this famous spot are other point and reef breaks, including several that are known for barrels. Be warned that this area is experienced-surfer territory, and the powerful waves aren't for beginners; if you're just learning to surf or are not yet confident on a board, you'll be better off elsewhere. You can usually surf year-round at Keramas, although the most consistent conditions are from April to November.

LISTINGS

Best Places for...

$ Budget $$ Midrange $$$ Top End

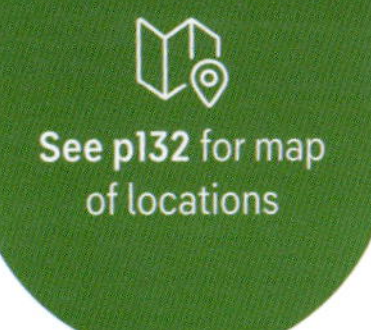

Eating

Restaurants with Views

Giri Carik $

13 B1

The uninterrupted view of Agung is hard to beat. Come for a drink, or for Balinese specials like *babi kecap* (pork with sweet soy sauce). *9am-9pm*

Blue Earth Village Restaurant $

14 F1

Begin your day with peaceful views of Agung and the ocean, plus excellent coffees, juices and healthy breakfast options. *7.30am-10pm*

Indonesian Meals

Warung Bu Jero $

see 10 D3

You'll find regular Indonesian fare at super-affordable prices, but it's worth splashing out on the succulent seafood. *9am-10pm*

Warung Mewali $

see 9 F1

A family-run warung (food stall) right on Amed beach. Gaze past fishing boats to the ocean while you sip cocktails and feast on seafood. *10am-9pm*

Bali Asli $$$

15 E2

The menu at this outstanding restaurant changes daily, always honouring the island's timeless culinary traditions. *8am-7.30pm*

Atmospheric Dining

Warung Seni Tejakula $

see 11 E1

A delight of a find, this small, creative cafe in Tejakula takes as much care with its healthy food as it does with its garden and decor. *9am-8pm*

Warung Cepik $

16 B2

There's a four-page vegan menu at this restaurant, which offers other meals, too. Tables have a relaxing paddy view. *7am-8.30pm*

Shopping

Traditional Textiles

Pertenunan Setia Cap Cili

17 B3

Founded in 1948, this third-generation factory has a large showroom where you can buy exquisite handwoven *endek* textiles. *9am-5pm Mon-Fri*

Cap Togog

see 17 B3

At one of Gianyar's last remaining shops and weaving factories, you can see the entire *endek* production process in action. *9am-5pm Mon-Fri*

Pelangi Traditional Weaving

18 C1

Shop for handwoven *endek* and *songket* fabrics, and look around the workshop to see women weaving and men tying designs onto the threads. *9am-5pm*

★ WORTH A TRIP

More to Do in Bali

Beyond the main coverage in this guide, there are still myriad more places of note, both on Bali and the nearby islands. Whether on a day trip or as part of a longer sojourn, the more notable areas of interest are detailed here.

PLANNING TIP
Hiring a car with driver, easily arranged through your accommodation, is the most comfortable way to explore beyond south Bali. Expect to pay upwards of 1,000,000Rp for a full day.

West Bali

Bali's true west, stretching from beyond Pura Tanah Lot to the ferry port for Java at Gilimanuk, remains dotted with corners where solitude is the norm. It's easy to find serenity amid its wild jungle, rice fields and charcoal-hued beaches.

Surfers hit the breaks at small beachside spots like **Balian Beach** (about 90 minutes' drive from central Canggu), where a small surfer community has sprung up with simple guesthouses and posher retreats. Further west, **Medewi** is even more remote, with guesthouses, resorts and some great places to eat. **Pura Rambut Siwi** is nearly as important as Pura Tanah Lot, but draws a fraction of the crowds.

Central Highlands

This misty, volcanic highland region lies within day-tripping distance from the south, but expect a long day out.

Hundreds scale active volcano **Gunung Batur** (1717m) daily to watch the sunrise from the rim of its caldera. It's roughly a three-hour drive from Canggu to reach the base of the climb. At Bedugal are the **Bali Botanic Garden** and the **Danau Beratan** lake with its sacred Hindu temple, **Pura Ulun Danu Bratan**.

Scan this QR code for information on boats to the islands.

Right: Pura Ulun Danu Bratan

DANIEL_FERRYANTO/SHUTTERSTOCK

DUDAREV MIKHAIL/SHUTTERSTOCK

The former Dutch hill station of **Munduk**, a hiking centre, has misty views down the hills to the north coast. In the shadow of dormant **Gunung Batukau**, you'll find one of Bali's most mystic temples, **Pura Luhur Batukau**. Just south, the UNESCO-listed **Jatiluwih rice terraces** bedazzle with cascades of green.

North Bali

The big draw north of the mountains is the incredible diving and snorkelling at **Pulau Menjangan**, in West Bali National Park. Arcing around a nearby bay, **Pemuteran** may be Bali's best beach town: a relaxed oasis with an artificial reef offering excellent snorkelling right offshore. In the middle of the north coast, **Lovina** is a sleepy beach strip with cheap hotels. Just east, museums and history await in **Singaraja**. Inland, waterfalls cascade down green hillsides thick with wild fruit trees and hiking trails.

Gili Islands

The Gili Islands are a trio of tropical islands with low-hanging palms and crystal-clear waters. Each is surrounded by lively reefs and caters to tourists, with scores of guesthouses, cafes and bars. All three islands are vehicle-free, and each has its own personality. The busiest, **Gili Trawangan** (Gili T), has all-night parties, while the quietest, pint-sized **Gili Meno**, maintains plenty of local character and tradition. **Gili Air** feels like a fusion of the other two.

Fast boats depart for the Gilis from Padangbai, Sanur and Serangan ports. All are required to make a detour to the port of Bangsal on Lombok. The trip from Sanur takes about 3½ hours.

NORTH BALI TIPS

Factor in a four-hour drive from the Canggu or Sanur areas to Pemuteran or about 3½ hours from Ubud. Most visitors stay in Pemuteran for at least a few nights, but it's easy to stay much longer, especially if you're a diver.

ISLAND-HOPPING

Many people choose to visit all three Gili islands, spending a night or town on each one. The best transport option is the public speedboats that run between the islands, usually hourly between 9am and 4pm – these cost 85,000Rp per person.

Left: Snorkelling at Gili Trawangan

Bali Toolkit

Pantai Suluban **(p84)**

SUN_SHINE/SHUTTERSTOCK

Family Travel

Travelling with children in Bali is an enriching experience. Everyone has a responsibility towards children here – kids of all ages will enjoy both the attention and the many diversions. Outdoor activities are a plus.

What to Pack

Supermarkets and stores stock almost everything you'll need – indeed, almost everything you'd find in similar shops at home. Nappies (diapers), baby food, packaged UHT milk, infant formula etc are easily purchased in Bali. Items to bring with you include a portable changing mat, car seat, favourite food and a sling or other type of baby carrier.

DINING WITH KIDS

Bali is so relaxed that kids can just be kids while eating out as a family. At many eateries, kids romp around nearby while their parents enjoy a meal. Kitchens will usually cater to fussy palates.

Best Regions for Kids

Seminyak Surf lessons and calm, breezy beach life, without the overlay of sleaze found in Kuta.

Sanur Beachside resorts, a reef-protected beach and many family-friendly activities.

Nusa Dua Huge resorts with kid-friendly programs and a reef-protected beach.

Ubud Walks in nature, monkeys, colourful markets and vibrant dance performances provide endless entertainment.

Stuff for Kids

Kids love Bali's many markets, where you can laugh at all sorts of novelties and souvenirs. Dance performances delight older kids.

Beach Safety

Always watch kids in the water. The ocean surrounding Bali is unpredictable, and lifeguards are rare.

Staying Safe

The facilities and safeguards that many parents regard as basic may not be present in Bali. Think balcony railings and pool fencing. The main danger to kids – and adults – is traffic and bad footpaths.

NAME/CREDIT

Accommodation

Bali has every kind of place to stay imaginable. Prices are often more reasonable than you'd expect, aside from busy times.

Where to Stay if You Love...

A Vibe

Canggu (p33) is packed with cool cafes, on-trend restaurants and boutiques galore. The beaches pulse with simple bars and huge clubs looking out over the surf.

We Love to Stay in...

Ubud (p115)
The famous town embraces visitors with a Balinese vibe that's more intense than other popular areas of the island. Nightly cultural shows, ricefield walks and excellent restaurants add to the appealing character. Family-run guesthouses offer lovely connections to local life, and eco-resorts fold you into the lush landscape.

Surf and Views

Uluwatu (p79) is home to Bali's most famous surf break, with white-sand beaches scooped from its lofty cliffs. Accommodation is delightfully idiosyncratic, although there are also lavish resorts.

HOW MUCH FOR A NIGHT IN

A hostel dorm bed **from US$13**

A boutique mid-range hotel **from US$70**

A lavish resort **from US$250**

Resorts

Nusa Dua (p91) and the neighbouring areas are lined with top-end resorts run by international brands, with hundreds of rooms and every possible amenity. They offer reliable and cloistered escapes.

Family-friendly Holidays

Sanur (p99) is the place for a relaxed holiday that also feels connected to Bali. Reefs protect the beach, which is lined with hotels of all types.

Buzz

Seminyak (p49) is the heart of South Bali tourism. It has a huge range of accommoda-tion, restaurants and bars abound, and you're never far from the beaches – and sunsets.

Food, Drink & Nightlife

Allergies & Intolerances

People with food allergies and intolerances should be extremely careful when eating in Bali. Problematic substances such as nuts (especially peanuts) are used as a base for many dishes, such as nasi campur (pictured), even if they aren't a featured ingredient. Kitchens aren't set up to have nut-free zones. However, international-style eateries in Cangguand Ubud, and some big resorts, may be more familiar with food sensitivities and vegan preferences.

WHEN TO EAT

Chefs and cooks go to markets in the morning to buy fresh produce, and prepare enough food to last all day. Meals are usually grabbed on the run and eaten when convenient. Visitors should follow local eating habits and enjoy anything at any time.

YOU WANT IT SPICY?

Food in Bali has been blandified to suit the perceived tastes of tourists. From the humblest market stall to the finest restaurant, no one wants tourists complaining about too much spice. So getting some fire in your meal requires work. Ask for 'Bali spicy' or 'pedas', though it still won't be as piquant as residents prefer.

Embrace Beer

It's safest to avoid ordering spirit-based drinks outside of high-end hotels and cocktail bars. Over the years, there have been a number of cases involving tourists who unknowingly ordered drinks made with home-made alcohol, or methanol, and either died or were permanently injured.

HOW TO... Pay the Bill

Generally, you'll need to ask for the bill or you'll be sitting at your table indefinitely. Catch your waiter's attention and say 'the bill tolong'.

Splitting the bill Sometimes possible, but don't bank on it. Tap and pay is increasingly available.

Tipping Only expected at high-end places but greatly appreciated by staff, where small amounts make a meaningful difference. Always tip in cash to your server (or place it in a staff tip-box) and aim for 10%. Paying cash and refusing change is a good way to tip.

PRICE RANGES

The following price ranges refer to the average cost of a main course.

$ under 70,000Rp

$$ 70,000–250,000Rp

$$$ 250,000Rp and up

OPENING HOURS

Cafes 8am to 9pm

Restaurants 8am or 11am to at least 9pm

Night Markets 6pm to 10pm

Going Out

Beer You can get a cold one almost anywhere in Bali. The ubiquitous convenience stores, beach vendors, cafes, restaurants and more sell beer any time they're open.

Wine and cocktails Higher-concept beach cafes, clubs and specialty venues will supply you, as will any place to eat that has a bar.

When to go Cafes tend to be open during daylight hours and early evening. Beach bars wait until closer to sunset (vendors take up the slack during the daytime). The big beach clubs go all day and then morph into proper clubs at night. Dance clubs hew closer to international standards, with some not getting going until after 11pm.

What to wear Beach venues are obvious – whatever you want. Elsewhere, a modicum of decency is necessary to avoid offence. No bathing suits or shirtless attire in cafes, restaurants and the like. Clubs may have stricter rules.

JAKUB JOZWIK/SHUTTERSTOCK

HOW MUCH FOR A

Top-end restaurant meal
250,000Rp+

Nasi campur
40,000Rp

Nasi goreng
50,000Rp

Babi guling
50,000Rp

Balinese coffee
10,000Rp

Cocktail
160,000Rp+

Jamu (herbal health drink)
20,000Rp

Fresh coconut water
15,000Rp

LGBTIQ+ Travellers

LGBTIQ+ travellers in Bali should follow the same precautions as straight travellers: no public displays of affection, although attitudes are usually relaxed.

Acceptance?

Bali in general is one of the most LGBTIQ-friendly places in Southeast Asia owing to the many ways it caters to a rainbow of visitors. Couples shouldn't expect any issues when checking into a room, and there is a large LGBTIQ+ expat community here. Many own businesses that – if not gay-specific – are gay-friendly. In South Bali and Ubud, couples have few concerns beyond remembering that the Balinese are quite modest. Public displays of affection by anyone are disrespectful to residents.

In 2022 Indonesia passed a morality law aimed at preventing sex outside of marriage, with Bali's governor clarifying that it is only enforceable if a 'parent, spouse or child' complains to the police.

Top LGBTIQ+ Areas

In general, Canggu, Seminyak, Uluwatu and Ubud are where LGBTIQ+ people can be the most open and comfortable, and where you'll see obvious signs of LGBTIQ+ life. Seminyak has a row of gay bars and clubs on Jl Camplung Tanduk.

LGBTIQ+ LEXICON

Gay men in Indonesia are referred to as *maho* or 'gay'; lesbians are *lesbi*. Many transgender people, particularly trans women, identify as *waria*, which comes from the words *wanita* (woman) and *pria* (man).

CHANGING ATTITUDES

A 2020 survey found only 9% of Indonesians agreed that homosexuality should be accepted, an increase from only 3% in 2013.

ROLAND MAGNUSSON/SHUTTERSTOCK

Resources

gayanusantara.or.id Indonesia's LGBTIQ+ community group. Focuses on social issues, government policy, support services, HIV prevention and more. • **Yayasan Gaya Dewata** Bali's oldest community-run LGBTIQ+ organisation works to prevent HIV and provide support services.

Health & Safe Travel

While Bali is generally safe, crimes do happen. Visitors also need to exercise a degree of caution in relation to their physical safety.

DRUGS

High-profile drug cases in Indonesia should dissuade anyone from getting involved with illicit drugs. Ecstasy tabs or a bit of pot have resulted in huge fines, multiyear jail sentences and even the death penalty. Cops pose as dealers and often bust foreigners for drugs, whether in clubs or private villas.

Water Safety

Ferries, ships and boats in Indonesia have a mixed safety record. Never assume any voyage will be safe, as crews may have little or no training, so use your common sense. While there are good operators on the waters around Bali, the lineup changes constantly. If a service or boat seems sketchy to you, go with a different operator. Try to get a refund, but don't risk your safety for the cost of a ticket.

Don't Drink the Water

Tap water in Bali is never safe to drink. Use filtered or bottled water.

QUICK INFO

Security

Keep an eye on your personal possessions wherever you are.

Drugs

Never allowed, and not worth the risk.

Alcohol

Always allowed.

Scams

Common scams:

- 'Mandatory' temple offerings (it's never mandatory).
- Scammers charging outrageous sums for 'repairs' to rental scooters. Document every scratch before setting off.
- Fake Gojek or Grab drivers. Always book via the app.
- Cashiers giving you the wrong change. Stay alert or use a card.

SWIMMING

Beaches are subject to heavy surf, strong currents and pollution. Swim between safety flags (if present) and know that lifeguards are uncommon. Stay away from open streams flowing into the surf.

Responsible Travel

Follow these tips to leave a lighter footprint, support local and have a positive impact on communities.

Community Tourism

JED (Jaringan Ekowisata Desa; Village Ecotourism Network) organises highly regarded tours of small Balinese villages, some overnight. Working with villages off the tourist routes, rural life, culture, farming and food are explored. All proceeds are returned to the communities. *jed.or.id*

Muntigunung is a community initiative that works to improve livelihoods through activities aimed at tourists in and around its namesake village in East Bali. Tours include food production, handicrafts and treks. *instagram.com/muntigunungcse*

Regenerative Rice

The **Astungkara Way** *(astungkaraway.com)* provides farmers with free training and support to transition to sustainable rice farming. Farm experiences near Ubud and multiday hikes support its work.

Sustainability

At the entrance to Seminyak's legendary **Desa Potato Head** (p54) read about how every aspect of its business is dedicated to sustainability.

Let Wildlife Be Wildlife

Reconsider swimming with captive dolphins, riding elephants and patronising attractions where wild animals are made to perform for crowds. These interactions have been identified by animal welfare experts as harmful to the animals.

FROM LEFT: TRY_MY_BEST/SHUTTERSTOCK, TEACHER PHOTO/SHUTTERSTOCK, CLAIRE ADAMS/SHUTTERSTOCK

Resources

- **keepbalibeautiful.com** Donate to community recycling programs.
- **facebook.com/kutabaliseaturtle** Join the turtle hatchery's next turtle release.
- **worldanimalprotection.org.au** Read up on responsible animal tourism in Bali.

CLEAN BALI'S RIVERS

Sungai Watch *(sungai.watch)* has identified over 350 illegal landfills in Bali and organises river cleanups to keep rubbish off the beaches. The organisation is expanding its work across Indonesia, and you can help out.

Be a Trash Hero

Join the **Trash Hero** *(trashhero.org)* volunteers who clean up garbage across Indonesia, and who partner with communities on education and sustainability projects that aim to reduce and better manage plastic waste in particular. There are chapters in Canggu, Sanur, Tabanan and Amed as well as on Gili Meno.

Climate Change & Travel

It's impossible to ignore the impact we have when travelling; Lonely Planet urges all travellers to engage with their travel carbon footprint, which will mainly come from air travel. While there often isn't an alternative, travellers can look to minimise the number of flights they take and use cleaner ground transport, such as trains. One proposed solution – purchasing carbon offsets – unfortunately does not cancel out the impact of individual flights. While most destinations will depend on air travel for the foreseeable future, for now, pursuing ground-based travel where possible is the best course of action.

The **UN Carbon Offset Calculator** shows how flying impacts a household's emissions:

The **ICAO's carbon emissions calculator** allows visitors to analyse the CO_2 generated by point-to-point journeys:

REFILL YOUR WATER BOTTLE

Avoid adding to Bali's waste crisis by refilling your reusable water bottle (always pack one) at your accommodation and at restaurants. Scan the QR code to find out where to refill your water bottle in Bali.

Accessible Travel

Accessibility Challenge

Bali is a difficult place for people with limited mobility, vision or hearing. Few buildings have access for people with disabilities. Expect high kerbs, few kerb ramps, badly maintained and crowded footpaths, and steps into many establishments. Help, however, is usually at hand, even if it may not be skilled.

Balinese Qualities

If formal accommodation for access needs is lacking in Bali, help is not. Residents are particularly ready to offer help to anyone in need of it. The island is also rich in sensory delights, whether by eye, ear, nose, taste or touch.

TEMPLES & SIGHTS

Steps are an integral aspect of every Hindu temple, meaning most Balinese shrines and sights are not accessible. Paved seaside walkways in Sanur and Kuta have braille but steps in Kuta complicate wheelchair access.

Accessible Activities

Waterbom Bali (p63) Offers discounted entrance for people with disabilities and carers, and much of the park is wheelchair-friendly.

Zero Gravity Diving *(zerogravitydivingbali.com)* Offers dives for qualified disabled divers as well as courses. In Sanur.

The resorts of **Nusa Dua** (p91) are designed and built to international accessibility standards. Throughout Bali, top-end resorts tied to international brands are the places to go for accessible rooms, barrier-free access around the property and other facilities to suit a range of needs. Elevators are standard and staff are trained to provide whatever assistance is needed, such as participating in activities. Referrals to businesses such as dive operators that can accommodate people with accessibility needs are also possible.

AIRPORT

Bali's Ngurah Rai Airport is modern and capable of catering to passengers with diverse needs. A Special Needs Service *(bali-airport.com/en/special-needs-services)* is provided to passengers. Reserve ahead.

Resources

baliaccesstravel.com A specialist travel agent providing accessible tours, accommodation, transport, equipment hire and licensed nursing services.

Nuts & Bolts

Opening Hours

Banks 8am–2pm Monday–Thursday, 8am–noon Friday, 8am–11am Saturday

Government offices 8am–3pm Monday–Thursday, 8am–noon Friday (although these are not standardised)

Restaurants and cafes 8am–9pm (open longer In busy areas)

Shops and services catering to visitors 9am–8pm

Rural shops and attractions 9am–dusk

QUICK INFO

Time zone
Central Indonesian Time (GMT/UTC plus eight hours)

Country code
+62

Emergency number
Police 110; Fire 113; Medical 119

Population
4.5 million

ELECTRICITY

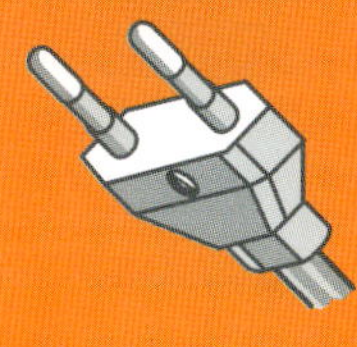

Type C
220V/50Hz

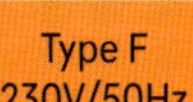

Type F
230V/50Hz

Toilets

Western-style toilets are common in tourist areas. In rural areas, toilets are porcelain holes in the floor with footrests on either side and a bucket of water for flushing.

Public toilets only exist at some attractions.

Public Holidays

Indonesia has a long list of national and religious holidays. The following are the most prominent in Bali.

Tahun Baru Masehi (New Year's Day) 1 January

Tahun Baru Imlek (Chinese New Year) Late January to early February

Nyepi (Day of Silence) February or March

Hari Buruh (Labour Day) 1 May

Hari Proklamasi Kemerdekaan (Independence Day) 17 August

Hari Natal (Christmas Day) 25 December

Dates change each year for the following Islamic holidays:

Isra Miraj Nabi Muhammad (Ascension of the Prophet Muhammad) Around January

Idul Fitri (End of Ramadan) February or March

Idul Adha (Islamic Feast of the Sacrifice) Around May

Muharram (Islamic New Year) Around June

Maulud Nabi Muhammad (Birthday of the Prophet Muhammad) Around December

Language

Basics

Hello.
Salam.

Goodbye. (leaving)
Selamat tinggal.

Goodbye. (staying)
Selamat jalan.

How are you?
Apa kabar?

I'm fine, and you?
Kabar baik, anda bagaimana?

Excuse me.
Permisi.

Sorry.
Maaf.

Yes.
Ya.

No.
Tidak.

Please...
Silahkan.

Thank you.
Terima kasih.

You're welcome.
Kembali.

Fast Phrases

Do you speak English?
Bisa berbicara Bahasa Inggris?

I don't understand.
Saya tidak mengerti.

What's your name?
Siapa nama Anda?

My name is ...
Name saya ...

Eating & Drinking

What's in that dish?
Hidangan itu isinya apa?

That was delicious.
Ini enak sekali.

Cheers!
Bersulang!

Bring the bill/check, please.
Tolong bawa kuitansi.

That was delicious.
Ini enak sekali.

a table ...
meja ...

- **at (eight) o'clock**
  pada jam (delapan)
- **for (two) people**
  untuk (dua) orang

I don't eat ...
Saya tidak makan ...

- **dairy products.**
  susu dan keju
- **fish**
  ikan
- **(red) meat**
  daging (merah)
- **peanuts**
  kacang tanah
- **seafood**
  makanan laut

Numbers

satu

2
dua

tiga

empat

lima

Good to Know

Indonesian, or Bahasa Indonesia, is the official language of Indonesia. It has approximately 220 million speakers, although it's the mother tongue for only about 20 million. Most people in Bali also speak their own indigenous language, Balinese.

Indonesian pronunciation is easy to master. Each letter always represents the same sound and most letters are pronounced the same as their English counterparts.

Indonesian, and its closest relative Malay, both developed from Old Malay, an Austronesian language spoken in the kingdom of Srivijaya on the island of Sumatra.

EMERGENCIES

Help!
Tolong!

Go away!
Pergi!

Call ...!
Panggil ...!

...a doctor
dokter

...the police
polisi

Signs

Buka Open
Dilarang Prohibited
Kamar Kecil Toilets
Keluar Exit
Masuk Entrance
Pria Men
Wanitai Women
Tutup Closed
Polisi Police
Rumah Sakit Hospital

Transport & Directions

Where's (the station)?
Di mana (stasiun)?

What's the address?
Apa alamatnya?

Can you show me (on the map)?
Bisa tunjukkan kepada saya (di peta)?

Please stop here.
Tolong, berhenti i sini.

BALI SLANG TO LISTEN OUT FOR

Alay Tacky, garish, drama queen
Basian Hangover
Jijay Disgusting, grotesque
Kimpoi Sexual intercourse
Koplak Silly
Pansi What the hell?

enam

tujuh

delapan

sembilan

sepuluh

Index

Sights p000 Map pages p000

See also separate subindexes for:
Eating p161
Drinking p161
Shopping p162

Eating

Drinking

Shopping

Send Us Your Feedback

We love to hear from travellers – your comments help make our books better. We read every word, and we guarantee that your feedback goes straight to the authors. Visit lonelyplanet.com/contact to submit your updates and suggestions.

Note: We may edit, reproduce and incorporate your comments in Lonely Planet products such as guidebooks, websites and digital products, so let us know if you are happy to have your name acknowledged. For a copy of our privacy policy visit lonelyplanet.com/legal.

Acknowledgements

Cover photograph: Balinese women at Hindu ceremony. Denis Moskvinov/Shutterstock

Back photograph: Thomas Beach (p87). Matheus Beltrame/Shutterstock

THIS BOOK

The 9th edition of Lonely Planet's Bali guidebook was researched and written by Sarah Reid, Jade Bremner, Narina Exelby, Mark Eveleigh, Marco Ferrarese and Leyla Rose. The previous edition was written by Ryan Ver Berkmoes. This guidebook was produced by the following:

Destination Editor
James Pham

Coordinating Editor
Michael Mackenzie

Cartographer
Julie Sheridan

Production Editor
Robin Yule

Image Researcher
Rita Harper

Cover Researcher
Katelyn Perry

Thanks to
Michelle Bennett, Melanie Dankel, Kate James, Alison Killilea, Helen Koehne, Saralinda Turner

Paper in this book is certified against the Forest Stewardship Council™ standards. FSC™ promotes environmentally responsible, socially beneficial and economically viable management of the world's forests.

Published by Lonely Planet Global Limited
CRN 554153
9th edition – Aug 2026
ISBN 978 1 83869 870 6

10 9 8 7 6 5 4 3 2 1
Printed in China